Beyond Devotionals: A 31-Day Deep Dive Into Aligning with God's Will

Yolanda Allen

Published by Iris Purple Moon Publishing, 2024.

While every precaution has been taken in the preparation of this book, the publisher assumes no responsibility for errors or omissions, or for damages resulting from the use of the information contained herein.

BEYOND DEVOTIONALS: A 31-DAY DEEP DIVE INTO ALIGNING WITH GOD'S WILL

First edition. January 4, 2024.

ISBN: 979-8989606122

Written by Yolanda Allen.

Table of Contents

To Malik, Ahmad, Kayla, Skylar, and Savannah: For whenever you feel lost and need a little direction. I love you.

To my siblings and cousins: Grandma instilled this in us a long time ago. I'm glad that we're each carrying on her legacy in our own way.

In memory of my momma...my number-one cheerleader. I miss you so much.

Within the music and melody lie the everlasting notes of love and friendship that bring harmony to my soul. Thank you.

Copyright Permissions

———

——————

When you pass through the waters, I will be with you; and when you pass through the rivers, they will not sweep over you. When you walk through the fire, you will not be burned; the flames will not set you ablaze.

Isaiah 43:2 NIV

When you're in over your head, I'll be there with you. When you re in rough waters, you will not go down. When you're between a rock and a hard place, it won't be a dead end—

Isaiah 43:2 MSG

Diving In: Your 31-Day Guide

───

Welcome, dear friend, to your journey beneath the surface. Born from my own personal quest to reconnect with God, *Beyond Devotionals: A 31-Day Deep Dive into Aligning with God's Will,* is an invitation for you to engage deeply with your faith, just as I did. It's a roadmap that I hope will illuminate your path as you navigate the complexities of your relationship with God.

This section is designed to help you navigate the way ahead, providing structure to your experiences and explorations. Here, each entry becomes an opportunity to explore faith, discover insights about yourself and find comfort during challenging times.

After countless devotionals that skim the surface, you've embarked on a journey that goes beyond. This is not your ordinary devotional; instead, it is an intensive study designed to take you beneath the surface of scripture, tradition, and personal reflection. We'll deep dive into the heart of God, seeking clarity in guidance, gratitude, and wisdom. With a commitment to understanding and application, you'll emerge transformed, equipped to align more closely with God's will.

In this exploration, as I alluded to earlier, you'll primarily focus on three foundational pillars: Guidance, Gratitude and Wisdom. While each day will center around one of these themes, you might find that some topics naturally interweave with other spiritual concepts. That's the intricate tapestry of God's word; threads from one area can often be pulled into another, enriching our understanding. So, even if a day's reflection might seem to branch out, trust that the overarching theme remains rooted in the primary pillars. My hope is that you embrace the fluidity of God's wisdom and see where it leads you.

As you embark on this trek, please remember that this guide is not just about completing tasks, adhering to a strict daily schedule or checking a box off your to-do list. While the structure is laid out as a day-by-day guide, it's perfectly okay if you find that you need more time to fully absorb and reflect on each day's topic.

For example, if Day 7's exploration of "The Greatness and Protection of Our God" draws you in and you feel compelled to spend several days delving into this theme, then I encourage you to do so. This book is yours...which means this journey is personal to Y-O-U. It is important to honor your own pace. If a particular topic or scripture requires more time for contemplation, prayer or application in your life, by all means, take that time. This deep dive is not a race; it's a journey of the heart and soul.

In this introductory section, let me provide an overview of what you can expect from each part of your journal. Each component serves a unique purpose, guiding you through a thoughtful and intentional exploration of the themes and lessons presented in the journal entry.

1. **FOCUS:** This is your starting point. It sets the stage by highlighting the theme explored in that entry. Whether it's about guidance, gratitude or wisdom, this is where your exploration begins.

2. **SONG:** Accompanying each day's theme is a song suggestion. While the song title and artist are provided, you won't find a direct link to the song included due to copyright reasons. An online search will easily lead you to it. You can listen before diving into the day's lesson, or you can listen afterward to reflect on what you just studied. Some find that playing the song while reading can be distracting. Choose whatever approach best enhances your experience. The song is meant to be an emotional and spiritual backdrop, helping to create the "mood for the day." There is no right or wrong way to use the song.

3. **INTRODUCTION:** This section sets the context for the chosen scripture. It offers a brief commentary or explanation to help you better understand the scripture's background, key themes and why it's relevant to our focus. As we delve into the reading, this introduction aims to enrich your understanding and guide your reflections.

4. **READING:** This is the heart of each entry. It presents a selected passage or scripture that provides wisdom and inspiration for your reflections.

5. **KEY PRINCIPLES:** The reading's main ideas, concepts or teachings are broken down here. You'll explore these essential lessons in the rest of the entry.

6. **CONCLUSION:** This is a thoughtful wrap-up of the scripture, highlighting its key messages and teachings. It offers a summary that encourages deeper reflection on the scripture's themes and relevance to our lives, helping us remember and appreciate the wisdom in the holy words.

7. **REFLECTION:** This is where you turn inward. Engage in personal introspection through thought-provoking questions or prompts tied to the entry's theme.

8. **PRAYER:** This is your quiet space for prayer or meditation. Use it to express gratitude, seek guidance, find comfort or simply connect with God.

9. **GOING DEEPER:** If you're ready to dive even further, this section awaits. While completely OPTIONAL, it is crafted to enhance your experience. You might find questions that echo earlier themes, but trust that they are designed to challenge you more than those questions found in the Reflection section. It's an invitation to a richer exploration.

10. **NAVIGATING YOUR JOURNEY:** Consider this your practical guide, offering tips, steps and recommendations to support your journey following each day's lesson.

BEYOND DEVOTIONALS: A 31-DAY DEEP DIVE INTO ALIGNING WITH GOD'S WILL

Each section within your journal entry is designed to guide you through a meaningful and transformative experience. Embrace the process, allow the words to resonate within you, and let the journal be a source of inspiration and guidance on your path of self-discovery and spiritual growth.

Author's Note: The creation of *Beyond Devotionals: A 31-Day Deep Dive into Aligning with God's Will* has been a heartfelt journey, inspired by my experiences in developing study guides for small groups in my local church. These humble efforts have been a part of my spiritual journey, and I've brought the same spirit of service and reflection to this book. While AI assisted in refining the final product, the structure and content are deeply rooted in my personal reflections and experiences and are my own. My hope is that this guide serves as a meaningful companion on your own journey of faith.

Understanding God's Will

———

Hey friend, just a quick note...

Understanding God's will is a journey that takes time, patience and openness. Remember, it *gradually* unfolds as you cultivate your spiritual awareness and deepen your relationship with God.

This journal, filled with reflections, prayers and prompts, is your toolkit for this quest. Approach it with an open heart and readiness for self-reflection. This process is continuous, but each step brings you closer to aligning your life with His will.

Now, let's discuss some strategies to assist you in discerning God's will:

- **PRAYER:** (Engage in conversations with God).

Spend time in prayer, seeking God's wisdom and guidance. Share your desires, concerns, and decisions with Him, and ask for His leading and clarity. Be open to hearing His voice through prayerful listening.

- **SCRIPTURE**: (Dive into God's Word for guidance and wisdom).

Study and meditate on the Word of God. The Bible is a rich source of guidance and wisdom. Pay attention to the principles, teachings, and examples in Scripture that align with God's character and values. They can provide a framework for discerning His will.

- **SEEK GODLY COUNSEL:** (Reach out to trusted mentors and advisors).

Seek the counsel of trusted mentors, pastors, or spiritual advisors who can offer wisdom and guidance. Surround yourself with wise, mature believers who can provide biblical insights and help you discern God's will.

- **LISTEN TO THE HOLY SPIRIT:** (Pay attention to the spiritual insights within).

Cultivate a relationship with the Holy Spirit, who dwells within believers. The Holy Spirit can guide and prompt you as you seek God's will. Tune in to the still, small voice within you, and be sensitive to His leading.

- **OPEN AND CLOSED DOORS:** (Watch for opportunities and obstacles; they can guide your path).

Pay attention to the opportunities and closed doors in your life. Sometimes, God's will becomes evident through the doors He opens or closes along your journey. Seek His guidance as you discern the paths that align with His purposes for you.

- **ALIGNMENT WITH GOD'S CHARACTER:** (Aim to reflect God's virtues in your actions).

Consider whether your actions, habits, and decisions align with the character of God as revealed in Scripture. Seek to honor Him in your choices and prioritize values such as love, humility, justice, and compassion.

Are you ready? Deep breath, now! Okay...let's plunge into this transformative journey together.

DAY 1: Bliss in Forgiveness: Embracing the Path of Confession and Redemption

---

FOCUS:

Guidance

SONG:

Firm Foundation (He Won't) – Cody Carnes

INTRODUCTION:

In Psalm 32, King David reflects on the joy of having one's disobedience forgiven and sins removed by the Lord. He shares the consequences of keeping sin hidden and the relief he experienced when he confessed and received forgiveness. David then emphasizes the importance of seeking God's guidance and trusting in Him, contrasting the sorrows of the wicked with the unfailing love surrounding those who put their trust in the Lord. Ultimately, David calls on everyone to rejoice in the Lord and find gladness in obeying Him with pure hearts.

READING:

Psalm 32 (TPT)

What bliss belongs to the one whose rebellion has been forgiven, those whose sins are covered by blood. What bliss belongs to those who have confessed their corruption to God! For he wipes their slates clean and removes hypocrisy from their hearts.

Before I confessed my sins, I kept it all inside; my dishonesty devastated my inner life, causing my life to be filled with frustration, irrepressible anguish, and misery. The pain never let up, for your hand of conviction was heavy on my heart. My strength was sapped, my inner life dried up like a spiritual drought within my soul.

Then I finally admitted to you all my sins, refusing to hide them any longer. I said, "My life-giving God, I will openly acknowledge my evil actions." And you forgave me! All at once the guilt of my sin washed away and all my pain disappeared!

This is what I've learned through it all: All believers should confess their sins to God; do it every time God has uncovered you in the time of exposing. For if you do this, when sudden storms of life overwhelm, you'll be kept safe.

Lord, you are my secret hiding place, protecting me from these troubles, surrounding me with songs of gladness! Your joyous shouts of rescue release my breakthrough.

I hear the Lord saying, "I will stay close to you, instructing and guiding you along the pathway for your life. I will advise you along the way and lead you forth with my eyes as your guide. So don't make it difficult; don't be stubborn when I take you where you've not been before. Don't make me tug you and pull you along. Just come with me!"

So my conclusion is this: Many are the sorrows and frustrations of those who don't come clean with God. But when you trust in the Lord for forgiveness, his wraparound love will surround you. So celebrate the goodness of God! He shows this kindness to everyone who is his.

Go ahead—shout for joy, all you upright ones who want to please him!

KEY PRINCIPLES:

1. **Joy in Forgiveness:** This Psalm underscores the deep-seated joy and relief derived from acknowledging our sins and receiving God's forgiveness. We unlock the door to inner peace and joy as we embrace this forgiveness.
2. **Consequences of Hidden Sin:** Highlighting the detrimental impact of unconfessed sins on our inner life, this Psalm encourages us to confront and acknowledge our wrongdoings rather than keep them hidden. The consequences of concealed sin can be devastating, leading to inner turmoil and spiritual drought.
3. **The Power of Confession:** In this Psalm, David extols the transformative power of confession. He shares how acknowledging his sins and refusing to hide them any longer led to their forgiveness and the dissolution of his inner pain and guilt. Confession, thus, emerges as a powerful tool for spiritual liberation and renewal.
4. **Trust in God:** The Psalm emphasizes the importance of trusting in God and seeking His guidance, promising His unfailing love and protection in return. When we place our trust in God, we are shielded from life's storms and are graced with His unwavering love.
5. **Rejoicing in God's Love:** The final principle invites us to express joy and gladness in the goodness and kindness of God. Rejoicing in His love serves to affirm His heart toward us and deepens our spiritual connection with Him.

CONCLUSION:

In Psalm 32, we journey with David from the burden of hidden sin to the liberating joy of forgiveness. This scripture offers us a profound glimpse into the healing power of confession and God's unbounded, forgiving love. It encourages us not to bury our sins but to bring them to the light, where God's love can cleanse and restore us.

David also urges us to trust God's guidance, promising us protection and a surrounding of unfailing love when we do. The Psalm then culminates in a call to celebrate God's goodness, a rejoicing rooted not just in our actions but in the merciful heart of God Himself. This scripture reminds us of the cleansing power of confession, the security of trust and the joy found in celebrating God's enduring love. As timeless as life-changing, this wisdom guides us toward a life of authenticity, trust and jubilation in God's love.

REFLECTION:

1. Think about a moment when you realized you had made a mistake that was previously unnoticed or hidden. Describe how acknowledging, confessing and seeking forgiveness for this mistake impacted your life.
2. Some believe that some secrets or sins should be 'taken to the grave.' How does this sentiment align or conflict with the message of confession and forgiveness in Psalm 32? How might withholding such secrets affect our inner lives?
3. Reflect on a time when you felt that God's guidance was leading you into unfamiliar or uncomfortable situations. How did you feel? What was your response? If there was resistance from you, how has your response to God's call evolved? What factors influenced your reaction?
4. Describe a time when forgiveness – either given or received – led to a profound sense of relief or joy, like what David expresses in this Psalm after his sins are forgiven. How did this experience of forgiveness shape your understanding or perspective of mercy and love?
5. Describe a moment when you experienced a deep sense of God's 'wraparound love'- as mentioned near the end of the scripture – especially during moments of seeking or receiving forgiveness. What did this experience feel like? How did it affect your perspective on love and forgiveness (either from God or from people)?

PRAYER:

Gracious God, I come to you with a humble heart, aware of the times I've fallen short and the forgiveness I need. I thank You for Your endless mercy, for always welcoming me with open arms whenever I come to You in confession. Teach me to be honest with myself and with You, to acknowledge my wrongdoings and seek Your forgiveness, knowing that Your love is greater than any mistakes I've made.

Lord, guide me when I find myself in unfamiliar situations, even when I'm tempted to resist Your call. Help me to trust You, to let go of my fears and doubts and to willingly follow Your lead, even when the path is not clear.

Let me always be mindful of Your 'wraparound love' surrounding me, especially during times of forgiveness. Fill my heart with Your love, that I may not only receive it but also share it with others.

Help me celebrate Your goodness every day, find joy in Your forgiveness, and live my life as a reflection of Your love. In all things, Lord, let Your will be done.

In Jesus' name, I pray. Amen.

GOING DEEPER:

1. David talks about his inner life being devastated before confession and speaks of relief and joy after. Can you identify any long-term effects – whether emotional, physical, or relational – that unconfessed mistakes have had on your life? How might confession and forgiveness lead to healing in these areas?

2. Trusting God can mean letting go of control, which can be scary. Are there parts of your life where you're trying to keep control instead of letting God guide you? What fears, lies or beliefs might be stopping you from trusting God with these parts of your life?

3. Forgiveness often results in a profound sense of relief or joy, as described in Psalm 32. But it can also be challenging, especially when we have been deeply hurt. Are there people in your life whom you find hard to forgive? Remember, forgiveness doesn't always mean reconciliation or letting someone back into your life. How might the perspective of God's 'wraparound love' assist you in extending forgiveness, and how might this shape your understanding of boundaries and reconciliation?

4. In the Old Testament, people used animal sacrifices to ask for forgiveness. But in the New Testament, we learn that Jesus' sacrifice covers our sins. How does this change show God's love and mercy?

5. David talks about the joy of being forgiven. But sometimes, even when God or people forgive us, we still face the results of our actions. Can you remember a time when this happened to you? How did it affect your view of forgiveness and responsibility?

6. Sometimes, we think the terrible things that happen to us are God punishing us. Does this idea match what you learned about God's love and forgiveness from the reading? How can we tell

the difference between God teaching us a lesson and just facing the results of what we did?

7. Have you ever felt so guilty that it was hard to believe you were really forgiven, either by God or by someone else? How could remembering God's all-surrounding love help ease those feelings?

NAVIGATING YOUR JOURNEY:

1. Acknowledge and confess wisely. Begin by acknowledging your wrongdoings and mistakes. Practice this as part of your daily prayer or meditation. If you share your confession with another person, do so wisely. Not everyone needs to know everything about you; not everyone can be trusted with your vulnerabilities. Choose a trusted spiritual advisor, mentor or friend who has shown themselves to be compassionate, understanding and trustworthy.

2. Embrace forgiveness. Learn to accept forgiveness from God and others. Remember, forgiveness doesn't just remove the burden of guilt; it brings joy and bliss. Spend time each day reflecting on the mercy and love you've received and let that feeling fill your heart.

3. Forgive yourself. Sometimes, the person we find hardest to forgive is ourselves. Remember that God's forgiveness extends to you as well. You are allowed to make mistakes and grow from them. Let go of guilt and embrace the opportunity to learn and grow.

4. Avoid self-martyrdom. Self-martyrdom is when you constantly see yourself as a victim and dwell excessively on your mistakes. This can lead to an unending cycle or trap of perpetual guilt and self-punishment, preventing you from moving forward. Holding onto guilt and refusing to forgive oneself can lead to a self-focused cycle that can hinder personal growth and strain relationships. Avoid falling into this trap after making a mistake. Remember, your mistakes do not define your worth! Embrace God's grace, forgive yourself and focus on growth and learning.

5. Trust in God's guidance. As we navigate life, there will be times when we feel God is leading us into unknown or uncomfortable situations. Trust that He knows the best path for you. Spend time in prayer and meditation, seeking His guidance for your journey. Surrender your worries and fears to Him, trusting that He is leading you toward growth and healing.

6. Explore the power of God's love. Remember, God's love is 'wraparound'—it always surrounds and supports you. Try to connect deeply with this loving presence during your prayers and reflections. Feel His love in your life and let it inspire your actions. Remember, you are loved unconditionally by God. His love is always there regardless of your past mistakes or current struggles. Let this love inspire and strengthen you on your journey toward forgiveness and healing.

7. Practice forgiving others. Forgiving others can be tough, especially when we've been deeply hurt. But as followers of Christ, we're called to extend the same mercy we receive. *"Forgive*

us the wrongs we have done as we ourselves release forgiveness to those who have wronged us." *(Matthew 6:12 TPT)*. Begin with small steps. Start by praying for those who have hurt you and ask God for the strength to forgive.

8. Understand that forgiveness does not negate consequences. Forgiveness does not always mean the immediate end of suffering or consequences. While God forgives us, we must sometimes deal with our actions' consequences. This isn't punishment but rather a natural result of our choices. When facing difficult consequences, use them as opportunities to learn and grow.

9. Celebrate God's goodness. Just like David, make it a habit to rejoice and celebrate God's love and mercy. This could be through worship, prayer or even simple acts of gratitude in your daily life. Find joy in the love of God and allow it to spread throughout all aspects of your life. This means allowing the joy and love of God to influence and be present in every part of your life – from personal relationships to work to how you spend your free time and make decisions. Live in a way that deeply infuses the joy that comes from God's love into your day-to-day existence.

Remember, these steps are not meant to be a checklist but a guide to help you on your spiritual journey. The path will look different for everyone, and that's okay. Trust in God's guidance and go at your own pace. God meets you where you are.

Day 2: A Song of Thanksgiving and Remembrance

FOCUS:

Gratitude

SONG:

Thank You – The Katinas

INTRODUCTION:

PSALM 136 IS A HYMN of thanksgiving to God for His deeds and His enduring love. The psalmist recounts the acts of God, from creation to deliverance from Egypt to provision in the wilderness, each time echoing the refrain, "His love endures forever." This psalm invites us to reflect on God's goodness and express gratitude for His unchanging, everlasting love.

READING:

Psalm 136 (NIV)

Give thanks to the Lord, for he is good. His love endures forever.

Give thanks to the God of gods. His love endures forever.

Give thanks to the Lord of lords: His love endures forever.

To him who alone does great wonders, His love endures forever.

Who by his understanding made the heavens, His love endures forever.

Who spread out the earth upon the waters, His love endures forever.

Who made the great lights—His love endures forever.

The sun to govern the day, His love endures forever.

The moon and stars to govern the night; His love endures forever.

17

To him who struck down the firstborn of Egypt His love endures forever.

And brought Israel out from among them His love endures forever.

With a mighty hand and outstretched arm; His love endures forever.

To him who divided the Red Sea asunder His love endures forever.

And brought Israel through the midst of it, His love endures forever.

But swept Pharaoh and his army into the Red Sea; His love endures forever.

To him who led his people through the wilderness; His love endures forever.

To him who struck down great kings, His love endures forever.

And killed mighty kings—His love endures forever.

Sihon king of the Amorites His love endures forever.

And Og king of Bashan—His love endures forever.

And gave their land as an inheritance, His love endures forever.

An inheritance to his servant Israel; His love endures forever.

He remembered us in our low estate, His love endures forever.

And freed us from our enemies. His love endures forever.

He gives food to every creature. His love endures forever.

Give thanks to the God of heaven. His love endures forever.

KEY PRINCIPLES:

1. **God's Enduring Love**: The psalmist repeatedly emphasizes that God's love endures forever. This love is not merely a feeling, but a steadfast commitment demonstrated through His actions throughout history. His love is eternal, unchanging, and reliable.
2. **Reasons for Gratitude:** There are countless reasons to be thankful to God: His goodness, His great wonders, His creation, His deliverance, His provision, His victory over enemies, His care for His people in their low estate, and His provision of sustenance. God's consistent, loving

actions give us endless reasons to express gratitude.

3. **Remembering God's Deeds:** The psalmist recounts various acts of God, reminding us of His power and love. Remembering God's deeds encourages gratitude and bolsters faith, particularly during challenging times.

CONCLUSION:

Psalm 136 provides a rich tapestry of God's enduring love and faithfulness, from the awe-inspiring creation of the heavens and earth to the life-sustaining care for every creature. This divine love, eternal and unchanging, punctuates every verse of the Psalm, a constant refrain that reassures and uplifts us.

The psalmist presents an array of reasons for gratitude, from the grandeur of God's wonders to His provision and care. These are not just historical events but timeless expressions of God's love, reminding us of our own reasons to give thanks in our lives.

Indeed, remembering God's deeds isn't simply an exercise in nostalgia; it's a powerful means to nourish our faith, fortify our spirits and embolden our gratitude, especially during difficult times. These accounts serve as touchstones of divine compassion and power that echo into our present experiences.

As we reflect on this psalm, let's allow its messages to echo in our hearts, affirming the unchanging love of God, His faithfulness and His ceaseless commitment to us. Let the repeated refrain, "His love endures forever," resonate within us, reassuring us of God's eternal, steadfast love. This, in turn, fuels our gratitude, shaping a heart of thanksgiving that recognizes and appreciates the magnitude of God's enduring love in every season of life.

REFLECTION:

1. How does the recurring phrase "His love endures forever" affect your perception of God's love? What does this phrase mean to you in the context of your personal experiences?
2. What are some specific instances in your life where you have experienced God's enduring love? How did these experiences shape your faith and gratitude?
3. Reflecting on the many reasons for gratitude mentioned in the Psalm, can you identify similar reasons for gratitude in your own life?
4. The psalmist recites God's deed to encourage gratitude and faith in himself and others. What are some significant "deeds" or actions God has done in your life that you can tell and be grateful for?
5. Psalm 136 encourages us to remember God's deeds, particularly in challenging times. Reflect on a difficult time in your life. How did remembering God's previous acts of love and/or

faithfulness help you during this period?

6. Consider the act of giving thanks as presented in these verses. How can you more intentionally incorporate gratitude into your daily spiritual practice?

PRAYER:

Dear Heavenly Father, in the quiet moments of my day, I pause to reflect on the depth and magnitude of Your enduring love. I am humbled by Your steadfast devotion and ceaseless care, so evident in my life and the world around me.

I marvel at Your creation - the vast skies, the brilliant sun, the shimmering stars - and I am reminded of Your greatness. Your love is woven into the very fabric of the universe, a testament to Your boundless compassion and mercy.

I remember when You carried me through trials and tribulations, Your love the beacon guiding me through the storm. Your unwavering presence has been my comfort; Your love, my refuge. And I am immensely grateful. I ask for a heart that continually recognizes these blessings and sings Your praises, for You are truly worthy.

Please help me to live in a manner that reflects my gratitude. Guide me to love others as You have loved me, to serve as You have served, and to extend the grace and kindness that You so generously shower upon me.

In Jesus' name, I pray. Amen.

GOING DEEPER:

Take a moment to personalize and reflect on what you have read and prayed:

1. The writer of this Psalm sees God's actions as proof of His ongoing love. Can you think of tough times in your life - past hardships - that, when you look back on them now, you see them as hidden gifts or lessons?
2. The theme of Psalm 136 is universal, applying to everyone. However, personal experiences with God can significantly vary. How would you comfort or advise someone who struggles to see God's love in their life?
3. The verses recount historical events to illustrate God's enduring love. How can we reconcile this with personal or societal events that seem contrary to this depiction of God's love?
4. In Psalm 136, God's love is depicted as always there and never changing. But there might be times when you felt God was far away or you wondered if He loved you. Can you think about

those times? How does it match up with the idea of God's unchanging love?

5. The act of giving thanks can significantly change how we see life. How could focusing on what you're grateful for, and what you're thankful for, potentially shift your perspective or attitude concerning a personal situation?

NAVIGATING YOUR JOURNEY:

When it comes to cultivating an attitude of gratitude and remembering God's deeds, here are a few suggestions:

1. Start from the last known point. If you ever feel distant from God, return to when you last remember feeling close to Him. Reflect on that time, seek Him there, and retrace your steps. This exercise can help you understand any changes and can guide you back into feeling His loving presence.

2. Express gratitude daily. Recognize and appreciate something you're thankful for each day, no matter how small. This simple habit can help foster a positive mindset and draw you closer to God's enduring love.

3. Maintain a gratitude journal. Document your thoughts, prayers and experiences that you're thankful for. When going through difficult times, your journal can remind you of God's unending blessings and love.

4. Connect with scripture. Dedicate time each day to read and reflect on God's Word. Focus on scriptures highlighting God's unwavering love and faithfulness to strengthen your faith during trials.

5. Pray for insight. In moments of doubt or during life's difficulties, pray for wisdom and understanding. Ask for the ability to discern God's love even amid hardships.

6. Serve others. Serving others allows you to see God's love in action and often provides fresh perspectives on your own circumstances. It can help uncover overlooked reasons for gratitude.

7. Celebrate God's love. Acknowledge God's love as manifested in His creation, His gifts and His daily provision for you. By celebrating His love, you become more aware of the everyday miracles around you.

Remember, the journey to fostering gratitude and experiencing God's love isn't always straightforward. It requires sincere reflection, steadfast faith and consistent practice. But as you navigate this path, know that each step brings you closer to experiencing His enduring love more profoundly. In good times and in trials, His love is constant, and gratitude becomes our compass guiding us back to Him

Day 3: Kingdom Revelations for Life's Journey

———

FOCUS:

Wisdom

SONG:

God I Look To You – Bethel Music & Jenn Johnson

———

INTRODUCTION:

PROVERBS 1 INTRODUCES us to the concept of wisdom and the importance of listening to instruction. The book, written primarily by King Solomon, is filled with valuable principles for everyday living. Solomon presents wisdom as a person calling out to us, inviting us to learn and grow. The wisdom of Proverbs encourages us to fear the Lord, understand that our actions have consequences and that ignoring wisdom leads to disaster.

READING:

Proverbs 1: 1-19 (TPT)

Here are kingdom revelations, words to live by, and words of wisdom given to empower you to reign in life, written as proverbs by Israel's King Solomon, David's son. Within these sayings will be found the revelation of wisdom and the impartation of spiritual understanding. Use them as keys to unlock the treasures of true knowledge. Those who cling to these words will receive discipline to demonstrate wisdom in every relationship and to choose what is right and just and fair. These proverbs will give you great skill to teach the immature and make them wise, to give youth the understanding of their design and destiny. For the wise, these proverbs will make you even wiser, and for those with discernment, you will be able to acquire brilliant strategies for leadership.

These kingdom revelations will break open your understanding to unveil the deeper meaning of parables, poetic riddles and epigrams, and to unravel the words and enigmas of the wise. We cross the threshold of true knowledge when we live in obedient devotion to God. Stubborn know-it-alls will never stop to do this, for they scorn true wisdom and knowledge.

Pay close attention, my child, to your father's wise words and never forget your mother's instructions. For their insight will bring you success, adorning you with grace-filled thoughts and giving you reins to guide your decisions.

When peer pressure compels you to go with the crowd and sinners invite you to join in, you must simply say, "No!" When the gang says - "We're going to steal and kill and get away with it. We'll take down the rich and rob them. We'll swallow them alive and take what we want from whomever we want. Then we'll take their treasures and fill our homes with loot. So come and join us. Take your chance with us. We'll divide up all we get; we'll each end up with big bags of cash!" - my son, refuse to go with them and stay far away from them.

For crime is their way of life and bloodshed their specialty. To be aware of their snare is the best way of escape. They'll resort to murder to steal their victim's assets, but eventually it will be their own lives that are ambushed. In their ungodly disrespect for God they bring destruction on their own lives.

KEY PRINCIPLES:

1. **The Fear of the Lord:** The reverence and respect we hold for God as the highest authority forms the foundation of all wisdom. Understanding God's supremacy is the first and fundamental step toward acquiring wisdom. Acknowledging His authority, we align our behaviors, decisions and attitudes harmoniously with His teachings and commands.

2. **The Consequences of Ignoring Wisdom:** Proverbs 1 underscores the perils of dismissing wisdom. Ignoring wisdom doesn't merely keep us stagnant; instead, it can lead us toward disaster. This principle is a serious warning, reminding us that embracing wisdom is not an optional preference but a critical choice that significantly influences our overall well-being.

3. **Teaching the Immature:** Proverbs offer a potent resource for educating the inexperienced and the young. This principle reflects the transformative potential of wisdom, demonstrating its power to guide, enlighten and mature those who engage with it. It underscores the importance of teaching wisdom from an early age to shape discerning individuals.

4. **Enhancing Wisdom and Discernment:** Wisdom isn't a static state but an ever-evolving trait that deepens and expands with time. This principle illustrates that even those already wise can benefit from continually engaging with wisdom. It contributes to a further sharpening of discernment, enhancing leadership capabilities and decision-making skills.

5. **Obedient Devotion to God:** True wisdom extends beyond intellectual understanding; it's rooted in a devoted relationship with God. This principle emphasizes that genuine wisdom and comprehension originate from obedience and heartfelt devotion to God. It's through this dedicated relationship that we access divine wisdom and guidance.

6. **The Pitfalls of Stubborn Resistance to Wisdom:** This principle highlights the importance of

self-awareness in our pursuit of wisdom. We must recognize and overcome any barriers we may unknowingly erect against wisdom. The key lies in humility and openness, acknowledging that continuous learning is an integral part of our spiritual journey.

CONCLUSION:

These verses teach us that wisdom is like a guiding light, helping us navigate life's twists and turns. It tells us that wisdom is always ready to help us if we're open to learning.

We are reminded that respecting God is the first step toward wisdom and that wisdom helps us grow and understand things better. It also points out that a strong relationship with God gives us insight that's deeper than just knowing facts.

We are warned that ignoring wisdom can lead to problems. It's not a neutral choice – if we turn away from wisdom, we're heading toward trouble.

In a nutshell, wisdom is not just a good trait to have – it's vital for living a good and enlightened life. As we ponder these teachings, let's aim to embrace wisdom and apply it to our everyday lives fully.

REFLECTION:

1. Reflect on the concept of wisdom as a person calling out, inviting us to learn and grow. How does this imagery resonate with your understanding of wisdom?
2. How has advice from your parents or mentors shaped your life? Are there words of wisdom you carry with you from them?
3. Think about when you felt pressured to go against your better judgment. How did you respond, and how has that shaped your understanding of wisdom?
4. How does your understanding of God's authority influence your daily decisions? Can you recall a recent decision that was heavily influenced by this understanding?
5. Solomon urges us to use wisdom as a guide in every relationship, whether romantic, family, friendships, acquaintances or professional. Reflect on your relationships. How can you apply wisdom to enhance these connections and interactions?
6. Wisdom in Proverbs is presented as a guiding and protective force. Consider times when wisdom has guided your decisions and helped to shield you from potential harm. How can you apply this protective wisdom more intentionally in the future?

PRAYER:

Heavenly Father, I stand before You today, recognizing how deep and wide Your wisdom spans. In the vast universe of Your creation, Your wisdom is the guiding star that leads me, instructs me and illuminates my path. Even amid chaos, confusion or uncertainty, Your wisdom remains a constant, a source of guidance and direction that I can always rely on.

Thank You, Lord, for making this wisdom accessible to me, whispering its truths to my heart, and using it to shape and mold me. I am in awe of its power – to transform, empower, and enlighten.

In those moments when I'm at the crossroads of life, when decisions feel heavy and pathways unclear, remind me of Your wisdom, Lord. Please help me lean on it, seek its counsel, and allow it to guide me in my interactions and relationships. May it serve as a beacon, leading me to fairness, justice and righteousness.

As I strive to embody the teachings of Solomon, teach me, Lord, not to hoard Your wisdom but to share it. Let me use Your wisdom as a tool for mentoring and teaching, for imparting understanding to those who seek it, for guiding the young and for enlightening those who may be lost.

I pray that Your wisdom penetrates every aspect of my life. May it enrich my personal journey and benefit those around me. May my life reflect the wisdom You have shared with me, serving as a testament to Your enduring love, mercy and wisdom.

In Jesus' name, I pray. Amen.

GOING DEEPER

1. The reading describes wisdom as calling out to us and offering guidance. How can you become more attuned to this call in your daily life? What specific steps could you take to be more receptive to the call?
2. Think back to a time when you followed advice that, looking back on it now, wasn't the best or wisest. How did that experience change the way you seek guidance or make decisions now?
3. The pitfalls of ignoring wisdom were illustrated earlier. Can you identify patterns or recurring themes in your life where you've ignored wisdom? What changes can you make to avoid these pitfalls in the future?
4. Think about how gaining more wisdom can make you a better leader in different areas of your life. How can you work on building this wisdom, and how might it change the way you lead?
5. Consider the idea that real wisdom comes not just from learning and thinking but also from having a close relationship with God. What actions can you take to get closer to God and learn more about His wisdom?

6. Solomon talks about how wisdom can cause significant changes and improvements. How can you use this ability of wisdom to encourage positive change in your community or in the lives of people around you?

NAVIGATING YOUR JOURNEY:

1. Embrace a teachable spirit. Start with humility, acknowledging that you don't have all the answers and that there's always something to learn. This doesn't mean devaluing your own knowledge or experience but rather being open to the wisdom others, especially those with more experience, can offer. Recognize that everyone, regardless of age or background, can teach you something valuable.
2. Mediate on God's Word. Spend time daily in scripture. Reading, reflecting and meditating on God's Word will enhance your understanding of His wisdom and strengthen your relationship with Him.
3. Cultivate discernment. Discernment is the ability to judge well. To cultivate it, ask God for His wisdom, particularly when facing challenging decisions or complex situations. Pray for the insight to understand His teachings, the courage to follow His directions and the discernment to distinguish between teachings rooted in God's wisdom and those that are not.
4. Appy wisdom to relationships. Reflect on how you can incorporate wisdom in your interactions with others. This could involve active listening, striving to understand before being understood or exhibiting more patience and kindness.
5. Share wisdom. Wisdom isn't solely for personal development; it's meant to be shared. Find opportunities to share the wisdom you've acquired with others in a respectful way. This could be through conversation, mentorship or simply by modeling wise behavior.

Wisdom is not a destination...it's a journey. By embracing humility, meditating on God's Word, cultivating discernment, applying wisdom in our relationships and sharing it with others, we navigate this journey guided by the powerful light of God's wisdom.

Day 4: Transformed Lives: Embracing Justice, Generosity and Sabbath Rest

---

FOCUS:

Guidance

SONG:

Way Maker – Sinach

INTRODUCTION:

ISAIAH 58:9B-14 PRESENTS a stirring call from God to His people, urging them to change their ways and to seek true righteousness. In these verses, the prophet Isaiah relays God's promises to guide and help those who remove oppression, false accusation, and malicious speech from their lives. Furthermore, the passage highlights the blessings that come from observing the Sabbath and delighting in it. This is not just about refraining from work; it's about honoring the day as holy, dedicated to the Lord.

READING:

Isaiah 58: 9b-14 (MSG)

If you get rid of unfair practices, quit blaming victims, quit gossiping about other people's sins, If you are generous with the hungry and start giving yourselves to the down-and-out, Your lives will begin to glow in the darkness, your shadowed lives will be bathed in sunlight. I will always show you where to go. I'll give you a full life in the emptiest of places—firm muscles, strong bones. You'll be like a well-watered garden, a gurgling spring that never runs dry. You'll use the old rubble of past lives to build anew, rebuild the foundations from out of your past. You'll be known as those who can fix anything, restore old ruins, rebuild and renovate, make the community livable again.

If you watch your step on the Sabbath and don't use my holy day for personal advantage, If you treat the Sabbath as a day of joy, God's holy day as a celebration, If you honor it by refusing 'business as usual,' making money, running here and there—Then you'll be free to enjoy God! Oh, I'll make you ride high and soar above it all. I'll make you feast on the inheritance of your ancestor Jacob. Yes! God says so!

KEY PRINCIPLES:

1. **Removing Oppression:** God calls us to remove the heavy chains of oppression, to stop exploiting others, and to do away with every form of prejudice. We are to actively seek justice and righteousness, aiding those in need and showing kindness to those around us.
2. **God's Guidance and Protection:** As we live out God's commands, He promises to guide us, to answer our prayers, and to protect us. God's guidance is promised to those who turn from wrongdoing, show compassion to the hungry, and aid those in misery.
3. **Observing the Sabbath:** There is a special blessing for those who observe the Sabbath by not pursuing their own interests and honoring it as a day dedicated to the Lord. The Sabbath is a time of rest and spiritual rejuvenation, and it brings delight and honor from the Lord.

1. **Rebuilding and Restoration:** God promises that His people will rebuild long-deserted ruins and restore communities. This promise of renewal and restoration reflects God's restorative power at work in the lives of His people, communities, and the whole world.

CONCLUSION:

Isaiah 58:9-14 prompts us to eliminate unfair practices, help those in need, and respect the Sabbath. Living out these teachings gives us a life illuminated with guidance, resilience and spiritual abundance. The passage also emphasizes the beauty of observing the Sabbath, treating it not as an obligation but as a joyful celebration. As we ponder these insights, let's recognize the profound influence of fairness, generosity and reverence for God's commandments. Upholding these principles can lead to personal fulfillment and contribute positively to the world around us.

REFLECTION:

1. What actions can you take to stop unfair practices, blaming victims or gossiping about others' sins in your daily life? How can you extend your generosity to those who are hungry or in need?
2. The concept of the Sabbath is vital in this passage. The Sabbath is a day set aside for rest and worship, a day to cease from regular work and focus on God. How do you understand the principle of the Sabbath, and how do you observe it? If you don't currently observe a Sabbath, what obstacles are in the way?

3. The passage promises guidance and protection from God. Can you recall when you felt this divine guidance and protection in your life?
4. What areas in your community could use some rebuilding and restoration? How could you contribute to this process?
5. This passage concludes with a promise of soaring high above all challenges. How does this promise resonate with your spiritual journey? What can you do to claim this promise in your life?

PRAYER:

Dear God, in a world that often feels divided and overwhelmed by strife, I come before you, longing for change, healing, and unity. Help me – and this world – seek true justice and righteousness, undeterred by the political games and distractions that so many get caught up in. God, empower me to be Your hands and feet, extending love and kindness to those around me, bringing Your light into the dark places.

Father, as I ponder the Sabbath concept, help me understand it deeply and implement it sincerely in my life. May I not see it as an obligation but as an opportunity – a gift of time to rest in Your presence, worship You, and recharge both physically and spiritually. May my observation of the Sabbath bring me closer to You and grant me the peace and rejuvenation my soul longs for.

Lord, You promise to guide and protect me, give me strength in the emptiest of places, and make me like a well-watered garden. I hold tightly onto these promises, trusting in Your faithfulness. Lead me as I seek to rebuild and restore the broken places in my life and the communities around me. Grant me Your wisdom and strength to make a positive difference, to bring healing and restoration wherever I go.

In Jesus' name, I pray. Amen.

GOING DEEPER:

1. Take some time to examine your day-to-day interactions. Are there any instances where you may be unwittingly contributing to the oppression or disadvantage of others? What concrete steps can you take to change this?
2. Reflect on the concept of the Sabbath as presented in the passage. How does it differ from your current practice, and what changes can you implement to make the Sabbath more of a delight than an obligation?
3. How can you involve others in your community in the work of justice and mercy? Are there initiatives or projects you can join or create to promote justice and aid the less fortunate?

4. God promises to guide us in the emptiest of places and provide a full life. Have you experienced times of emptiness? How have you seen God's guidance during these times, and how did it affect your spiritual journey?

NAVIGATING YOUR JOURNEY:

Implementing Isaiah 58:9-14 can be challenging but rewarding. Here are some steps to guide you.

1. Start small. Choose one specific action to address each week. It could be anything from avoiding gossip to setting time aside on the Sabbath specifically for rest and worship.
2. Reach out. Identify people or organizations in your community who are working for justice and lend a hand. Their work can guide and inspire you.
3. Set boundaries. On the Sabbath, resist the temptation to do work-related activities. Instead, spend the day on activities that refresh your spirit and strengthen your relationship with God. Or try to create quiet time where you unplug from electronic devices.
4. Identify your personal Sabbath. If you can't take an entire day off, carve out a dedicated time each day for rest and spiritual reflection. If setting aside a designated Sabbath time seems overwhelming, start small, then gradually increase this time as you become more comfortable with the practice. Remember that the Sabbath is about rest and connection with God, not perfection or strict rules.
5. Reflect and adapt. Regularly review your actions and attitudes. If certain behaviors continue to be challenging, seek guidance from trusted spiritual mentors, professional counselors or through prayer.
6. Seek and give support. Share your journey with others. Your experiences can encourage them, and their insights may help you see things from a different perspective.

Remember, every small step toward justice, generosity and honor for God's commandments brings you closer to experiencing His guidance, protection and abundance in your life. Stay committed and be patient with yourself throughout this journey.

Day 5: Joyful Prayers – Embracing Gratitude in Every Season

FOCUS:

Gratitude

SONG:

I've Got Joy – CeCe Winans

INTRODUCTION:

IN 1 THESSALONIANS 5:16-18, the Apostle Paul provides clear instructions for living a life that is pleasing to God. He emphasizes the importance of always being joyful, constant prayer, and being thankful in all circumstances. These commands aren't conditional or subject to change based on our situations or feelings. Paul reveals that this is God's will for us in Christ Jesus, meaning that embracing joy, prayer, and gratitude is integral to our Christian journey.

READING:

1 Thessalonians 5:16-18 (NLT)

Always be joyful. Never stop praying. Be thankful in all circumstances, for this is God's will for you who belong to Christ Jesus.

KEY PRINCIPLES:

1. **Always Be Joyful:** Joy is different from happiness, which is often dependent on circumstances. The joy Paul refers to is a deep-rooted, unshakeable sense of contentment and delight in God's goodness and faithfulness. This type of joy transcends our situations or feelings and is available to us in all circumstances through Christ Jesus.

2. **Never Stop Praying:** Paul encourages us to maintain an ongoing conversation with God. This doesn't mean we must be on our knees all day, but it suggests an attitude of constant communication and dependence on God. It's about acknowledging His presence and guidance

in all aspects of our lives.

3. **Be Thankful in All Circumstances:** This command can be challenging, especially when facing trials. Yet, Paul doesn't say we should be thankful *for* all circumstances but *in* all circumstances. This means recognizing God's goodness and grace at work, even in our difficulties, and expressing gratitude for His presence and provision.

CONCLUSION:

1 Thessalonians 5:16-18 outlines three critical practices for living a life pleasing to God: maintaining joy, sustaining prayer and cultivating thankfulness, regardless of our circumstances. These practices aren't merely suggestions, but rather, they reflect God's will for us. They call for an attitude shift, requiring us to look beyond our situations and feelings, focusing instead on God's goodness, grace and unfailing presence in our lives. In doing so, we can better navigate life's complexities with spiritual fortitude, hope and gratitude.

REFLECTION:

1. What does it mean to you to "always be joyful"? How can you maintain joy, even in challenging times?
2. In what ways do you "never stop praying"? How can you cultivate an ongoing conversation with God in your daily life?
3. How do you practice thankfulness in all circumstances? What helps you to focus on God's goodness and grace, even amidst trials?
4. How have these joyfulness, prayer and gratitude practices shaped your relationship with God and others?
5. How can you apply Paul's instructions in 1 Thessalonians 5:16-18 more fully in your life? What changes might you need to make?

PRAYER:

Heavenly Father, today I stand before you with an open heart, ready to lean more into your teachings. Guide me as I strive to cultivate a joy that doesn't waver with life's circumstances. Help me to foster an unbroken line of communication with You, not just in moments of need but in every breath I take.

When challenges arise, teach me to be thankful, to find grace amidst the trials and continually see the workings of Your divine plan. May my life be a testament to Your enduring love and goodness.

In Jesus' name, I pray. Amen.

BEYOND DEVOTIONALS: A 31-DAY DEEP DIVE INTO ALIGNING WITH GOD'S WILL

GOING DEEPER:

1. How has experiencing joy in God's presence helped you endure a difficult situation in the past? How could you share this with someone who might need encouragement right now?
2. Is there a particular time of day or activity where you feel particularly close to God? How could you leverage these moments for deeper prayer and connection?
3. When you're in the middle of a challenging situation, what strategies could you employ to shift your focus and find reasons to be thankful?
4. Who in your life models a lifestyle of joy, prayer and thankfulness? What can you learn from them?

NAVIGATING YOUR JOURNEY:

When it comes to personalizing the lesson and reflecting on how to cultivate a lifestyle of joy, prayer, and gratitude, here are a few suggestions:

1. Create 'Joy Moments'. Intentionally set aside moments in your day for joy. This could involve reading a Bible verse that brings you joy, spending time with someone who makes you smile, taking time to reflect on God's goodness, etc.
2. Consider starting a prayer journal where you can write down your prayers, thoughts and revelations throughout the day. This will keep you in constant communication with God and serve as a reminder of God's faithfulness when you look back.
3. Begin or end your day by listing three things you're thankful for. It could be as simple as a warm meal or a call from a friend. This practice can shift your focus from the day's challenges to God's grace and provision.
4. There may be times when you feel distant from God or unsure about what to say. It's okay to start small. Begin by telling God how you feel and asking for His help to open your heart again. Remember, there is no pressure to say the 'right' things. God values your honesty and willingness to reconnect.
5. Share and learn. Find a mentor or friend to share this journey with. They can provide advice, encouragement and share their experiences, making your journey less overwhelming and more enriching.

Remember, every small step toward joy, continuous prayer and thankfulness brings you closer to aligning with God's will for your life. Stay the course, and you will see the transformative power of these practices in your life. Through it all, know that God is patient and loving, always ready to listen and guide you through your journey.

Day 6: The Treasure of Wisdom – A Path to Happiness and Abundance

---

FOCUS:

Wisdom

SONG:

Every Prayer – Israel Houghton and Mary Mary

INTRODUCTION:

Proverbs 3:13-18 is a praise of wisdom and understanding. It illustrates wisdom's value as far greater than precious jewels or anything one desires. Wisdom is depicted as a tree of life to those who lay hold of her and are supported by her. These verses highlight the immeasurable wealth and happiness that come with wisdom and understanding and the peaceful, pleasant paths they provide.

READING:

Proverbs 3:13-18 (AMP)

Happy [blessed, considered fortunate, to be admired] is the man who finds [skillful and godly] wisdom, And the man who gains understanding and insight [learning from God's word and life's experiences], For her profit is better than the profit of silver, And her gain better than fine gold. She is more precious than rubies; And nothing you can wish for compares with her [in value]. Long life is in her right hand; In her left hand are riches and honor. Her ways are highways of pleasantness, and all her paths are peace. She is a tree of life to those who take hold of her, And happy [blessed, considered fortunate, to be admired] is everyone who holds her tightly.

KEY PRINCIPLES:

1. **The Value of Wisdom:** Wisdom is more valuable than precious stones or any material wealth. Its benefits surpass any earthly riches or desires. Wisdom's worth is incalculable and invaluable, providing spiritual riches that are everlasting and much more fulfilling.
2. **Abundance and Honor:** Wisdom brings abundant life and honor. With wisdom comes longevity and honor, offering a reward far more significant than material wealth. The

possession of wisdom signifies a life enriched with respect, dignity, and a meaningful existence.

3. **Wisdom is a Tree of Life:** Wisdom is described as a tree of life that nourishes and supports those who embrace it. Those who hold on to wisdom are nourished by its fruits, bringing a sense of fulfillment, peace, and happiness.

4. **Peaceful and Pleasant Paths:** Wisdom leads to paths of peace and pleasantness. The journey of wisdom is one of peace and joy, free from strife and turmoil. It brings tranquility and contentment, creating a fulfilling and satisfying life.

CONCLUSION:

Proverbs 3:13-18 beautifully encapsulates the significance and supreme value of wisdom. It encourages us to seek and treasure wisdom above all material wealth because its rewards are far greater – longevity, honor, peace and happiness. Wisdom isn't just an asset; it's described as a life-giving tree, offering nourishment to those who hold it tightly. The journey of wisdom might not always be easy, but it's assured to be peaceful and pleasant, leading us to a meaningful existence. The passage calls us to recognize the unmatched value of wisdom and invites us to prioritize the pursuit of wisdom in our lives.

REFLECTION:

1. What does comparing wisdom to precious stones and material wealth reveal about its importance in your life?
2. How have you experienced the abundance and honor that come with gaining wisdom in your own life?
3. In what ways have you experienced wisdom as a tree of life, providing you with nourishment and support? Reflect on life's path. How has wisdom helped you navigate your journey with peace and pleasantness?
4. How are you actively seeking wisdom in your life? What steps could you take to "hold her tightly"?

PRAYER:

Dear God, thank You for the gift of wisdom, more precious than earthly riches. Please help us to understand its supreme value and to pursue it wholeheartedly. Grant us the wisdom to navigate life's complex paths with peace and pleasantness. May we hold onto wisdom tightly, allowing it to nourish us, just as a tree of life would.

As we walk through life, let our steps be directed by Your wisdom, resulting in an enriched life of respect, dignity and a deeper understanding of Your word.

BEYOND DEVOTIONALS: A 31-DAY DEEP DIVE INTO ALIGNING WITH GOD'S WILL

In Jesus' name, I pray. Amen.

GOING DEEPER:

1. Can you share a time when you chose wisdom over material wealth? How did that decision impact your life?
2. The passage states, "Her ways are highways of pleasantness, and all her paths are peace." Reflect on this in the context of your life. How has wisdom guided you to peace and pleasantness?
3. Consider the metaphor of wisdom being a "tree of life." How does this imagery resonate with your understanding and experience of wisdom?
4. How can you better incorporate the pursuit of wisdom into your daily life? Are there specific actions or habits you might need to change?

NAVIGATING YOUR JOURNEY:

1. Reflect on your priorities. Are you seeking wisdom with the same determination as you seek material wealth? Consider how you might realign your priorities to value wisdom above all else.
2. Recall instances where wisdom has guided you to make beneficial decisions. Use these experiences as reminders of wisdom's value when faced with new challenges.
3. Regularly immerse yourself in God's Word, the source of wisdom. Spend dedicated time studying, reflecting and praying for increased understanding.
4. Seek the counsel of wise individuals in your life. They can offer valuable insights and perspectives from their own journeys of wisdom.
5. Practice gratitude for the wisdom you've gained through life's experiences. Recognize the growth you've achieved and be encouraged that you're on a path of peace and pleasantness.

As you journey on this path of wisdom, remember that each step, even the smallest one, brings you closer to a life that's more fulfilling, peaceful and aligned with God's purpose for you. Keep seeking, keep learning and keep growing in wisdom.

Day 7: The Greatness and Protection of Our God

FOCUS:

Guidance

SONG:

Thy Word – Amy Grant

INTRODUCTION:

Psalm 48 reminds us of God's unending guidance. It presents God as our eternal guide, who will lead us until the end of our days. This passage assures us of God's commitment to guide us through life's twists and turns, offering a sense of comfort and peace in our journey.

READING:

Psalm 48 (NLT)

How great is the LORD, how deserving of praise, in the city of our God, which sits on his holy mountain! It is high and magnificent; the whole earth rejoices to see it! Mount Zion, the holy mountain, is the city of the great King! God himself is in Jerusalem's towers, revealing himself as its defender.

The kings of the earth joined forces and advanced against the city. But when they saw it, they were stunned; they were terrified and ran away. They were gripped with terror and writhed in pain like a woman in labor. You destroyed them like the mighty ships of Tarshish shattered by a powerful east wind.

We had heard of the city's glory, but now we have seen it ourselves— the city of the LORD of Heaven's Armies. It is the city of our God; he will make it safe forever.

O God, we meditate on your unfailing love as we worship in your Temple. As your name deserves, O God, you will be praised to the ends of the earth. Your strong right hand is filled with victory. Let the people on Mount Zion rejoice. Let all the towns of Judah be glad because of your justice.

Go, inspect the city of Jerusalem. Walk around and count the many towers. Take note of the fortified walls, and tour all the citadels, that you may describe them to future generations. For that is what God is like. He is our God forever and ever, and he will guide us until we die.

KEY PRINCIPLES:

1. **God's Greatness and Strength:** Psalm 48 talks about how amazing and strong God is. It shows us His mighty presence, His rule over all things and how He protects us.
2. **God's Constant Love:** It underlines God's unfailing love that never ends. This love is something we think deeply about and celebrate when we worship. It gives us comfort and makes us feel safe.
3. **God's Fairness:** The Psalm is a joyful celebration of God's fairness. It encourages all the towns in Judah to be happy because God always makes fair decisions.
4. **Sharing the Greatness of God:** The Psalm encourages us to observe and think deeply about the evidence of God's greatness in our surroundings, much like one would do when going around the city of Jerusalem. It emphasizes the importance of not just recognizing and appreciating God's works but also sharing these experiences with future generations. This serves as a reminder for us to actively communicate the manifestations of God's greatness in our everyday lives.

CONCLUSION:

Psalm 48 is a beautiful song of praise for God's majesty, unfailing love, and justice. It celebrates God's powerful presence, reflected in the greatness of His holy city, Jerusalem. But, beyond the grandeur and glory, the Psalm speaks to the heart of believers who seek to understand and communicate God's wonders to future generations. It encourages us to meditate on His unfailing love, find joy in His justice and share our observations with others.

In the journey of faith, however, there can be times when life doesn't seem fair, and we struggle with feelings of confusion and doubt. It's important to remember in these moments that it's okay that we wrestle with such sentiments. They don't make us less faithful. Instead, wrestling can signify a deepening relationship with God as we seek to understand His justice in a world that often seems unjust. As we meditate on God's love, celebrate His justice and share His greatness, let us also be honest with ourselves and God about our struggles and doubts. For it's through this honesty that our faith is tested, strengthened and matured.

REFLECTION:

1. What feelings or thoughts come up for you when you reflect on the greatness of God, as described in this Psalm?
2. How do you usually express your awe or praise for God's majesty and power? What might be

some new ways you could celebrate His greatness?

3. What does God's unfailing love mean to you personally? How has this love been evident in your life?

4. How have you experienced God's justice or seen it in the world around you?

5. At times, life can seem unfair. How do you reconcile these feelings with your faith in God's justice?

6. What ways can you share with others about the great things God has done in your life, as the Psalmist suggests?

PRAYER:

Dear God, I thank you for Your majesty, unfailing love, and justice. As I meditate on Your greatness, help me better understand Your ways and Your works.

I acknowledge, Lord, that there are times when I struggle with confusion and doubt, especially when life seems unfair. Help me to wrestle with these feelings in a way that deepens my relationship with You and strengthens my faith. Remind me of Your constant presence and unfailing love, even amid my doubts.

Guide me as I seek to honor You with my life, express my praise and share Your greatness with others.

In Jesus' name, I pray. Amen.

GOING DEEPER:

1. Reflect on a time when you felt life was unfair. How did you cope with this feeling? What role, if any, did your faith play in this situation?

2. In what ways can you see God's unfailing love in your life, especially during times of hardship or uncertainty?

3. Consider the notion of God's justice. How do you perceive it in a world that often seems unjust?

4. How does acknowledging God's greatness and unfailing love influence your perception of life's difficulties?

5. Music and poetry have long been used to express feelings of awe and praise for God. Do you use these or other creative outlets to express your faith? How do they help you connect with God?

6. How can you share the great things God has done in your life with others?

NAVIGATING YOUR JOURNEY:

1. Take some time each day to meditate on God's greatness and unfailing love. This can be done through prayer, reading scriptures or simply quiet contemplation.
2. Reflect on your experiences of God's justice. If you feel that life is unfair, try writing about these feelings in a journal. This can help you to express and understand your emotions better.
3. Seek to express your praise for God's majesty and power through creative means. This could be through music, art, writing or any other creative outlet you enjoy.
4. Look for ways to share the great things God has done in your life with others. This could be through conversations with friends, sharing in a group or even through social media.
5. When wrestling with doubt or confusion, don't hesitate to seek support. Contact trusted friends, family members, a spiritual mentor or a professional counselor. There is no shame in seeking help. In fact, acknowledging you need support and taking steps to get it is a sign of strength and wisdom. Sharing your struggles can often bring comfort and new perspectives.

Remain patient with yourself as you navigate your feelings and continue your faith journey. Remember, it's okay to wrestle with feelings of unfairness. This doesn't make you less faithful but signifies a deepening relationship with God. Be open to His leading, rely on His wisdom, and trust in His eternal guidance.

Day 8: Harmony in Christ: Cultivating Peace, Thankfulness and Unity

---

FOCUS:

Gratitude

SONG:

Thank You Lord - Don Moen

INTRODUCTION:

COLOSSIANS 3:15-17 highlights the profound impact gratitude can have on our lives. As we immerse ourselves in these teachings, we are invited to consider how maintaining a thankful heart can genuinely transform our interactions with each other and with God. This passage not only gives us practical guidance on living in harmony with others but also challenges us to let our lives be a continuous song of thanksgiving.

READING:

Colossians 3:15-17 (MSG)

Let the peace of Christ keep you in tune with each other, in step with each other. None of this going off and doing your own thing. And cultivate thankfulness. Let the Word of Christ—the Message—have the run of the house. Give it plenty of room in your lives. Instruct and direct one another using good common sense. And sing, sing your hearts out to God! Let every detail in your lives—words, actions, whatever—be done in the name of the Master, Jesus, thanking God the Father every step of the way.

KEY PRINCIPLES:

1. **The Peace of Christ:** The peace that Christ gives should guide us and keep us in harmony with one another. His peace sets the tone for our interactions and keeps us united in purpose and spirit.

2. **Cultivating Thankfulness:** We are called to cultivate a heart of gratitude, being thankful in all

circumstances. This sense of thankfulness should be a constant presence in our lives, reflecting our recognition of God's goodness and mercy.

3. **The Word of Christ:** The Word of Christ should be free to move and work in our lives. It should instruct and guide us, influencing our thoughts, words, and actions.

4. **Every Detail in the Name of Jesus:** Everything we do, whether in word or action, should be done in the name of Jesus. This means that our lives should reflect Him and His teachings, and we should always give thanks to God through Jesus.

CONCLUSION:

Colossians 3:15-17 emphasizes the foundational role of Christ's peace in aligning our actions and interactions with others. It implores us to cultivate gratitude, let God's word guide us, and reflect Christ in every aspect of our lives. It encourages us not just to read or hear God's word, but to let it have the 'run of the house,' influencing our actions, words and attitudes.

The message is clear: When Christ's peace dwells in us, we can harmoniously align our actions with His teachings, using good common sense to guide our decisions. This passage urges us to let every detail of our lives, from words to actions, be done in Jesus' name, maintaining a heart of gratitude to God throughout our journey.

REFLECTION:

1. How has the peace of Christ influenced your relationships and interactions with others?

2. What practices help you cultivate a heart of gratitude? How can you be more thankful in your daily life?

3. How has the Word of Christ shaped your thoughts, words, and actions? How can you allow it to have more influence in your life?

4. In what ways do you strive to do everything in the name of Jesus? How can you better reflect Him in your life?

5. What does it mean to you to thank God every step of the way? How can you incorporate this into your life?

6. Which verse or part of the passage resonated with you the most? Why did it stand out, and what significance does it hold for your life and faith journey?

PRAYER:

Dear Lord, Your peace is a precious gift that harmonizes my heart with others and guides me in unity. Help me to live in tune with Your peace, letting it shape my interactions and decisions. Teach me to cultivate a heart of gratitude, finding reasons to give thanks in every circumstance.

Lord, may Your word have the run of my life. Let it guide my actions, mold my thoughts and influence my words. Help me to reflect Your love, mercy and grace in everything I do. And, in moments of celebration or challenge, remind me to do everything in Your name.

I pray that my heart sings to You, Lord, expressing my love, trust and praise. Let my life be a melody of faith, resonating with the rhythm of Your grace. In every detail of my life, may I honor You and thank You every step of the way.

In Jesus' name, I pray. Amen.

GOING DEEPER:

1. Consider your 'house'—your life, mind and heart. In what areas do you need to give God's Word more room? How can you intentionally make space for it in your daily routine?
2. Reflect on a situation where you found it hard to maintain the peace of Christ. How could you have approached it differently? How can you prepare for similar situations in the future?
3. Singing is mentioned as a way to express our hearts to God. How does music or worship impact your relationship with God? Remember, it's not about having a perfect voice but expressing our heart to God. Can you think of ways to incorporate this more in your daily life, perhaps through listening to worship music, humming a tune or even simply reading and meditating on the lyrics of hymns or worship songs?
4. How does cultivating gratitude change your perspective on challenges or difficult situations? Share a specific instance where being thankful shifted your outlook.
5. Can you identify any habits or actions in your life that are not done in the name of Jesus? How can you consciously aim to align these aspects with His teachings?

NAVIGATING YOUR JOURNEY:

1. Make a daily habit of acknowledging the peace of Christ in your life. You could do this through prayer, journaling, or meditation.
2. Cultivate gratitude by keeping a thankfulness journal. Each day, write down something you're thankful for.
3. Engage with God's Word. Read scripture daily and reflect on how it can be applied to your life.
4. Find ways to reflect Christ in your daily actions. This could be as simple as practicing kindness, patience or serving others.
5. Incorporate worship into your daily routine. This could be through music, prayer or acts of service.

Always remember your journey is unique and special. Be patient with yourself and trust that each step is leading you closer to God.

Day 9: Discovering the Path of Understanding

FOCUS:

Wisdom

SONG:

You Know Better – MercyMe

INTRODUCTION:

PROVERBS 2:1-11 IMPLORES us to seek wisdom and understanding as one would search for a hidden treasure. It urges us to value wisdom and knowledge, promising they will serve as a shield, guarding our paths and protecting us from harm. This passage underscores wisdom's protective and guiding power, asserting its essential role in leading a righteous life.

READING:

Proverbs 2:1-11 (AMP)

My son, if you will receive my words and treasure my commandments within you, So that your ear is attentive to [skillful and godly] wisdom, And apply your heart to understanding [seeking it conscientiously and striving for it eagerly]; Yes, if you cry out for insight, And lift up your voice for understanding; If you seek skillful and godly wisdom as you would silver, And search for her as you would hidden treasures; Then you will understand the [reverent] fear of the Lord [that is, worshiping Him and regarding Him as truly awesome] And discover the knowledge of God. For the Lord gives [skillful and godly] wisdom; From His mouth come knowledge and understanding. He stores away sound wisdom for the righteous [those who are in right standing with Him]; He is a shield to those who walk in integrity [those of honorable character and moral courage], He guards the paths of justice, And He preserves the way of His saints (believers). Then you will understand righteousness and justice [in every circumstance] And integrity and every good path. For skillful and godly wisdom will enter your heart, And knowledge will be pleasant to your soul, Discretion will watch over you, Understanding will guard you.

KEY PRINCIPLES:

1. **The Pursuit of Wisdom:** The quest for wisdom requires an intentional and diligent search, much like seeking a hidden treasure. It demands attention, respect, and a longing to understand more deeply.
2. **The Protective Power of Wisdom:** Wisdom acts as a shield, guarding our paths and protecting us from harm. It directs us toward righteousness and away from destructive ways.
3. **Wisdom as a Divine Gift:** Wisdom is a divine gift from God, who generously imparts it to those who earnestly seek it. From His mouth comes knowledge and understanding, guiding us in our daily lives.
4. **Wisdom and Understanding Lead to Righteousness:** Understanding and wisdom lead to righteousness, integrity, and justice, providing a moral compass to navigate life's complexities.

CONCLUSION:

Proverbs 2:1-11 is a refreshing call to the active pursuit of wisdom. It assures us that the quest for wisdom is rewarding but requires our proactive involvement – it is not a passive gift. Wisdom, here, is portrayed not merely as a personal attribute but a divine one, given by God and deeply intertwined with moral integrity. The virtues of righteousness, justice and integrity are promised to those who earnestly seek and treasure wisdom. In essence, this passage inspires us to live a life driven by wisdom, one that respects the awesomeness of God and cherishes His teachings. It's a journey toward wisdom, which brings personal growth and serves as a protective shield in our lives.

REFLECTION:

1. Consider the effort you put into gaining wisdom. How do you actively seek wisdom in your life, and how can you increase your efforts in this pursuit?
2. In what ways have you experienced the protective power of wisdom? Reflect on instances when wisdom has guided you away from harmful paths.
3. How do you seek wisdom from God? What practices or actions help you to connect more deeply with God to receive His wisdom?
4. Reflect on the link between wisdom and righteousness in your life. How has wisdom helped you to understand and pursue righteousness, integrity and justice?

PRAYER:

Dear God, I desire to embrace the wisdom that comes from You. Help me value and seek Your wisdom above all else, just as I would a precious treasure. I yearn for Your wisdom to fill my heart and guide my steps. I know Your wisdom will act as a shield, protecting and guiding me in Your righteousness.

Help me to understand and pursue justice, integrity and righteousness through Your wisdom. I trust that with Your wisdom within me, knowledge will become pleasant to my soul, discretion will watch over me, and understanding will guard me.

Thank you for Your promise of Your wisdom and protection. I commit to seeking You and Your wisdom every day.

In Jesus' name, I pray. Amen.

GOING DEEPER:

1. Reflect on a specific situation where you had to make a decision, and you sought God's wisdom. How did seeking wisdom influence the outcome?
2. How does actively seeking wisdom from God influence your perspective on situations around you? How does it affect your choices and decision-making processes?
3. What challenges do you encounter in your pursuit of wisdom? How can you overcome these obstacles to seek wisdom with more determination?
4. Wisdom is closely related to understanding and righteousness. Explore the influence of wisdom on your actions and character. How does it shape your responses to different situations?

NAVIGATING YOUR JOURNEY:

1. Start with a personal inventory. Where in your life do you feel a strong need for wisdom? Reflect on current decisions or challenges and consider how godly wisdom could influence your choices.
2. Brainstorm specific habits or actions that reflect wisdom and can be integrated into your life, like relationships, decision-making and personal growth.
3. Dive deeper into the Bible and your prayer life. Look for passages that focus on wisdom and its benefits and make these a central part of your study. In your prayers, be open and honest with God about your desire for more wisdom and understanding.
4. Put your wisdom into action: This could involve daily reading of a Proverb, seeking advice from individuals you consider wise or taking quiet moments to reflect on life's experiences from a wisdom-seeking perspective.
5. Build a support network. Surround yourself with other believers who can support and encourage your wisdom journey. Engage in discussions and shared learning with others who also want to grow in wisdom. Lean on each other for accountability and mutual

encouragement.

Remember, wisdom doesn't come instantly—it requires continuous, consistent pursuit. But the rewards are worth it. As you journey, remember that God is with you, ready to impart His wisdom to those who earnestly seek it.

Day 10: Trusting in the Lord: Finding Peace in His Promises

FOCUS:

Guidance

SONG:

I Trust You – James Fortune & FIYA

INTRODUCTION:

PSALM 37:1-11 EXPLORES how God guides us in a seemingly unfair world. This passage challenges us to shift our focus from worrying about others to trusting God's wisdom. It's a journey that asks us to be patient and humble, promising that God's guidance is there for those who choose this path.

READING:

Psalm 37:1-11 (AMP)

Do not worry because of evildoers, Nor be envious toward wrongdoers; For they will wither quickly like the grass, and fade like the green herb.

Trust [rely on and have confidence] in the Lord and do good; dwell in the land and feed [securely] on His faithfulness. Delight yourself in the Lord, And He will give you the desires and petitions of your heart. Commit your way to the Lord; Trust in Him also and He will do it.

He will make your righteousness [your pursuit of right standing with God] like the light, And your judgment like [the shining of] the noonday [sun].

Be still before the Lord; wait patiently for Him and entrust yourself to Him; Do not fret (whine, agonize) because of him who prospers in his way, Because of the man who carries out wicked schemes. Cease from anger and abandon wrath; Do not fret; it leads only to evil. For those who do evil will be cut off, But those who wait for the Lord, they will inherit the land.

For yet a little while and the wicked one will be gone [forever]; Though you look carefully where he used to be, he will not be [found]. But the humble will [at last] inherit the land And will delight themselves in abundant prosperity and peace.

KEY PRINCIPLES:

1. **Trust in the Lord:** God calls us to put our complete trust in Him, not to be envious or anxious about the deeds of evildoers. By trusting God, we acknowledge He is in control and His ways are best.
2. **Delight in the Lord:** Taking delight in God means finding joy and satisfaction in our relationship with Him. When we do this, God promises to give us the desires of our hearts.
3. **Commit Your Ways to God:** When we commit our plans and desires to God, He promises to act on our behalf, bringing our righteousness to light.
4. **Patience and Rest:** We're encouraged to rest in the Lord and to patiently wait for Him to act. We should not fret over those who seem to succeed in their wicked ways, for their success is short-lived.
5. **The Promise to the Meek:** God promises that the meek will inherit the land and enjoy abundant peace. This echoes the teachings of Jesus in the Beatitudes.

CONCLUSION:

Psalm 37:1-11 assures us that when we put our faith in the Lord, practice patience, and align our actions with righteousness, we are on a path to lasting peace and prosperity. It cautions against envy toward those who appear to prosper by wrongful means, urging instead to cultivate a fulfilling relationship with God and rest in his divine justice.

Particularly notable in this scripture is the emphasis on meekness. Often misconstrued in society as weakness or passivity, meekness is quite the opposite. It's an exercise of controlled strength. It's about being humble and gentle yet firm, especially when faced with adversity. It speaks of a quiet confidence in God's sovereignty and justice, of active submission to His guidance.

Choosing to embrace meekness means responding with grace and humility, even when we possess the power to react otherwise. It embodies a deeper trust in God's plan over our own strength. The Psalm promotes the virtues of meekness and promises a special blessing for those who adopt it. In seeking to embody meekness in our daily lives, we deepen our reliance on God and open ourselves to his life-changing guidance.

REFLECTION:

1. In what areas of your life do you need to trust God more? Reflect on circumstances where you've been anxious or worried instead of trusting God.
2. What does it mean to you to delight in the Lord? How can you cultivate a deeper joy and satisfaction in your relationship with God?
3. How can you commit your ways more fully to God? Are there any areas of your life that you're holding back from Him?
4. Where must you exercise more patience and rest in God's timing? Consider situations where you may have acted hastily or felt impatient.
5. How can you embody the meekness that God promises to bless? Reflect on ways you can cultivate humility and gentleness in your life.

PRAYER:

Dear Heavenly Father, thank You for Your promise to guide and direct my life. I choose to trust in You and not to be anxious about the success of the wicked. Help me to find joy and satisfaction in my relationship with You, knowing that as I delight in You, You will give me the desires of my heart.

Lord, I commit my plans and my life to You. Please guide me in all my ways and let my righteousness shine like the light. Teach me to be patient and to rest in Your perfect timing, knowing that Your ways are higher than mine.

Help me be meek and humble so that I may inherit the land and enjoy the peace that You promise. Thank You for Your guidance and love in my life. In Jesus' name, I pray. Amen.

GOING DEEPER:

1. Can you recall a specific situation where you felt God was guiding you? How did that experience affect your trust in His wisdom?
2. "Delighting in the Lord" is a deeply personal experience. Can you describe a moment when you felt a deep joy and satisfaction in your relationship with God? What made that moment special?
3. Trusting God often means giving Him control over all areas of our lives. Is there an aspect of your life where surrendering control feels challenging? Why do you think that is, and what might help you entrust this area to God?
4. The pace of our modern world often encourages haste and quick solutions. Can you remember a situation where waiting on God's timing proved to be the best course of action? How did that experience shape your understanding of patience?
5. God values meekness, a trait often undervalued in our society. Can you share an instance

where embracing humility and gentleness led to a positive outcome? How might this understanding of meekness change how you approach situations in your life?

NAVIGATING YOUR JOURNEY:

1. Start each day with a moment of trust. Share our worries with God and ask for His guidance for the day ahead. Remember, each day is a new opportunity to trust Him more – or again.
2. Seek to find delight in the Lord in your everyday activities. Whether during a quiet moment of prayer, in the beauty of nature, or in a kind act from a stranger, recognize God's hand in these joyful moments.
3. Make a conscious effort each day to commit your ways to the Lord. This could be as simple as making choices that honor Him or as significant as making a life-changing decision in faith.
4. Choose a situation each week where you can intentionally practice patience. Maybe it's allowing someone else to go first, waiting a little longer before making a decision, or simply taking a deep breath when you feel rushed.
5. Actively seek opportunities to practice humility and gentleness. This could be in your words, your actions or your thoughts. Remember, meekness isn't weakness but a controlled strength that reflects God's love.

Remember, growth and change don't happen overnight. It's about taking small, consistent steps toward trust, delight, commitment, patience and meekness. God is without in every step of this journey, cheering you on as you grow closer to Him.

Day 11: Praise and Worship – Celebrating the Lord's Goodness

FOCUS:

Gratitude

SONG:

10,000 Reasons (Bless the Lord) – Matt Redman

INTRODUCTION:

TODAY, WE DELVE INTO the beautiful Psalm 100, a Psalm of thanksgiving. This Psalm invites us to come into God's presence with joyful songs, thanks, and acknowledging He is good. The psalmist emphasizes the eternal nature of God's steadfast love and faithfulness, encouraging us to express gratitude for His unchanging character and endless mercy.

READING:

Psalm 100 (NIV)

Shout for joy to the Lord, all the earth. Worship the Lord with gladness; come before him with joyful songs. Know that the Lord is God. It is he who made us, and we are his; we are his people, the sheep of his pasture. Enter his gates with thanksgiving and his courts with praise; give thanks to him and praise his name. For the Lord is good and his love endures forever; his faithfulness continues through all generations.

KEY PRINCIPLES:

1. **Shout for Joy to the Lord:** The Psalmist invites us to express our joy and adoration for God openly and loudly, showcasing our love and gratitude for Him to all the earth.
2. **Enter His Gates with Thanksgiving:** This line suggests that we should approach God with a spirit of gratitude. It's a reminder to acknowledge and appreciate His goodness, mercy, and love, both in prayer and in our daily lives.
3. **The Lord's Love Endures Forever:** The Psalmist highlights the eternal nature of God's love.

No matter our circumstances, we can be assured that God's love for us is unchanging and everlasting.

CONCLUSION:

Psalm 100 is a powerful invitation to celebrate the Lord's goodness, love and faithfulness through joyful worship and gratitude. It is a powerful reminder of our identity as God's creation and as the sheep of His pasture, implying His gentle guidance, protection and care for us.

This scripture summons us to acknowledge God's sovereignty and love, encouraging us to respond with enthusiastic praise and thanksgiving. It assures us of the enduring nature of His love and faithfulness, providing us with a hopeful perspective that spans across generations.

As we continue our journey, let's carry the spirit of this psalm with us, approaching each day with a heart full of thanksgiving and a voice ready to sing joyful songs to the Lord. Let's celebrate the Lord's enduring love and goodness, remembering that we are His people, forever under His faithful watch.

REFLECTION:

1. Think about the joyful worship described in this Psalm. How can you incorporate this spirit of joy and gladness into your worship and daily life?
2. This scripture identifies us as 'the sheep of His pasture.' What does this picture or image mean to you personally? How does it shape your understanding of your relationship with God?
3. 'Enter his gates with thanksgiving and his courts with praise.' How can you bring a sense of gratitude into your daily encounters with God? Can you think of specific ways to express your thanks to Him?
4. Reflect on the phrase, 'his love endures forever; his faithfulness continues through all generations.' How have you experienced God's enduring love and faithfulness in your life?
5. This Psalm invites us to 'know that the Lord is God.' What does this statement mean to you? How does this knowledge impact your faith and how you live out your faith daily?

PRAYER:

Dear Heavenly Father, I come before You with a heart filled with joy and thanksgiving. I am grateful for the assurance that You are God, the creator who crafted us, and the shepherd who guides and protects us.

Teach me, Lord, to embrace the spirit of Psalm 100, to worship You with gladness, and to express my gratitude for Your enduring love and faithfulness. Let my life be a joyful song that honors You and reflects my appreciation for Your goodness.

Help me to enter each new day with a thankful heart, acknowledging Your loving-kindness that continues through all generations. May my actions and words be a testament to Your enduring love and faithfulness.

In Jesus' name, I pray. Amen.

GOING DEEPER:

Take a moment to personalize and reflect on what you have read and prayed:

1. Explore the picture of being 'the sheep of His pasture' further. This is a metaphor, like a word picture in which you describe something by using an image or idea that's something else. In what ways do you see God as your shepherd? How does this image help you trust Him more?
2. 'Shout for joy to the Lord, all the earth.' Think about what this command means for the global Christian community. How can you join with believers worldwide to shout for joy to the Lord?
3. There might be times when it feels challenging to perceive God's enduring love and faithfulness. Can you recall such a moment in your life? How did you navigate it and what helped you reconnect with your faith and relationship with God in general?
4. The Psalm ends with the affirmation that God's 'faithfulness continues through all generations.' Consider your role in passing on the testimony of God's faithfulness to the next generation. What steps can you take to fulfill this role?
5. How can you cultivate a daily attitude of worship, thanksgiving and praise as described in Psalm 100, regardless of your circumstances?

NAVIGATING YOUR JOURNEY:

When it comes to personalizing the lesson and reflecting on how to cultivate a lifestyle of joy and gratitude, here are a few suggestions:

1. Make it a daily habit to offer praise to God. It could be when you wake up, during a break in your day or before you go to sleep. Make this time intentional and focused.
2. Start a gratitude journal where you jot down what you're thankful for each day. This practice can help you 'enter His gates with thanksgiving,' as the Psalm advises.

3. Join others in worship, whether in person at church, online or with a group of friends. Worshipping in a community can enhance your sense of joy and connection.

4. Music has the power to lift our spirits and focus our minds on God. Find worship songs that resonate with you and incorporate them into your daily routine.

5. Regularly reflect on how God's faithfulness has manifested in your life. This can bolster your trust in His enduring love and guidance.

As you embark on these practices, remember that this is a journey, not a destination. Progress may be slow, and some days may be more challenging than others, but don't lose heart. Keep in mind that God's love endures forever, and His faithfulness continues through all generations. He is your constant companion on this journey, guiding, protecting and loving you every step of the way.

Day 12: Embracing Instructions for Life's Journey

―――

FOCUS:

Wisdom

SONG:

Yahweh – Maverick City Music

――――――

INTRODUCTION:

PROVERBS, THE BOOK of wisdom, provides practical insights and guidance for living a life that pleases God. In Proverbs 4:1-13, Solomon, the wisest man who ever lived, urges us to pursue wisdom and understanding. He assures us of wisdom's immense value and benefits, encouraging us to prioritize it above all else.

READING:

Proverbs 4:1-13 (NIV)

Listen, my sons, to a father's instruction; pay attention and gain understanding. I give you sound learning, so do not forsake my teaching. For I too was a son to my father, still tender, and cherished by my mother. Then he taught me, and he said to me, "Take hold of my words with all your heart; keep my commands, and you will live. Get wisdom, get understanding; do not forget my words or turn away from them. Do not forsake wisdom, and she will protect you; love her, and she will watch over you. The beginning of wisdom is this: Get wisdom. Though it cost all you have, get understanding. Cherish her, and she will exalt you; embrace her, and she will honor you. She will give you a garland to grace your head and present you with a glorious crown." Listen, my son, accept what I say, and the years of your life will be many. I instruct you in the way of wisdom and lead you along straight paths. When you walk, your steps will not be hampered; when you run, you will not stumble. Hold on to instruction; do not let it go. Guard it well, for it is your life.

KEY PRINCIPLES:

1. **Wisdom is Invaluable:** Solomon instructs us to prioritize wisdom above all else. He suggests

that wisdom and understanding are worth more than any material possessions we could ever accumulate.

2. **Wisdom Protects and Honors:** Wisdom serves as a protective shield, guiding us to make the right decisions and avoid pitfalls. Additionally, those who embrace wisdom will be honored and exalted.

3. **Wisdom Leads to Life:** Solomon emphasizes that wisdom is not only a pathway to a successful and prosperous life but is, in fact, life itself. He urges us to cling to wisdom, reminding us that it is vital to living a meaningful and fruitful life.

CONCLUSION:

Proverbs 4:1-13 invites us to cherish wisdom as the guiding light for a fulfilling life. It elevates the pursuit of wisdom and understanding to the highest priority, declaring that they are worth investing our all. This passage doesn't merely depict wisdom as something to acquire but illustrates it as a protector, an enhancer of our lives, and a harbinger of honor.

The sage father emphasizes the importance of holding on to wise teachings and internalizing them. Wisdom is not a passive asset but an active guiding principle. It safeguards our journey, ensuring we don't stumble as we tread along life's path.

This passage compels us to value wisdom and understanding, seek them persistently, and integrate them into our everyday actions and decisions. When we do, we find that wisdom is not just about knowledge; it's about creating a life of purpose, stability and honor.

REFLECTION:

1. How have you personally experienced the protective power of wisdom in your life? Can you recall a situation where wisdom guided your decisions and kept you from harm or error?

2. Consider the phrase: "Though it cost all you have, get understanding." What does this mean to you in practical terms? Are there areas in your life where you need to invest more time or resources to gain understanding?

3. Reflect on the teachings or wise instructions you've received. How well have you guarded these teachings, and how have they shaped your life's journey?

4. How does the imagery of wisdom gracing your head with a garland and presenting you with a glorious crown resonate with you? What do these images signify for you in your pursuit of wisdom?

5. In what ways can you actively 'cherish' and 'embrace' wisdom in your daily life? How might this devotion to wisdom affect your actions, decisions and relationships?

BEYOND DEVOTIONALS: A 31-DAY DEEP DIVE INTO ALIGNING WITH GOD'S WILL

PRAYER:

Dear God, with an open heart, I come before You today seeking Your wisdom and understanding. Help me to value Your teachings as precious treasures, cherishing them as the guiding light for my life's path.

I pray for the courage to seek wisdom, even when it requires effort and sacrifice. May I always remember that true wisdom and understanding come from You, and it is more valuable than any earthly riches.

In times of confusion or uncertainty, remind me to turn to Your wisdom for guidance. Help me listen attentively to Your instruction, guard it well, and let it shape my decisions and life.

As I seek wisdom, I pray for Your protection and guidance. I trust in Your promises that when I walk in the way of wisdom, my steps will not be hampered, and when I run, I will not stumble.

Thank You for the gift of wisdom and the promise of Your guidance. I pray for a heart that is ever open to Your instruction and a spirit that cherishes Your wisdom.

In Jesus' name, I pray. Amen.

GOING DEEPER:

Take a moment to personalize and reflect on what you have read and prayed:

1. The scripture talks about wisdom as if it's a person who can guide and protect us. How does thinking about wisdom in this way change how you see its role in your life?
2. The passage emphasizes the pursuit of wisdom, even at a significant cost. Consider a time when you had to sacrifice something valuable (time, resources, relationships) to gain wisdom or understanding. What did you learn from this experience?
3. 'Cherish her, and she will exalt you; embrace her, and she will honor you.' This verse suggests a give-and-take relationship between you and wisdom. How does this back-and-forth show up in your life?
4. Wisdom is said to keep us safe and prevent us from stumbling in life. Think about a time when being wise helped you through a challenging situation or a big decision.
5. How can you ensure you're putting a high value on wisdom in your everyday life? How might this help you grow closer to God, the source of all wisdom?

NAVIGATING YOUR JOURNEY:

In the quest for wisdom and understanding, here are some helpful practices:

1. Make a conscious effort to seek wisdom in all areas of your life. Ask yourself, "What is the wise thing to do?" before making decisions.
2. Seek wisdom from those around you. This could be friends, family, mentors or spiritual leaders. Listen to their experiences and learn from their insights.
3. It is not enough to gain wisdom; we must also apply it. As you navigate your daily life, look for opportunities to put your wisdom into action.
4. Reflect on the wisdom you gain by thinking about how it has impacted your day and how you can use it moving forward.

Remember, gaining wisdom is a process. Be patient with yourself and trust God's timing as you grow in wisdom and understanding.

Day 13: Wholehearted Trust – Guided by God's Voice

FOCUS:

Guidance

SONG:

Voice of Truth – Casting Crowns

INTRODUCTION:

PROVERBS 3:5-6 SPEAKS directly to our need for trust and reliance on God, especially in a world that often urges us to lean on our own understanding. Its simplicity makes its message profound – a reminder to trust God wholeheartedly and not rely solely on our reasoning or intuition. The scripture further encourages us to seek God's voice in every aspect of our life, understanding that He is the ultimate guide who keeps our path straight and true.

READING:

Proverbs 3:5-6 (MSG)

Trust God from the bottom of your heart; don't try to figure out everything on your own. Listen for God's voice in everything you do, everywhere you go; he's the one who will keep you on track.

KEY PRINCIPLES:

1. **Trust God Wholeheartedly:** Trusting God isn't merely an intellectual agreement but a heart commitment. We are to trust God from the bottom of our hearts, going all in with our faith in His wisdom, goodness, and faithfulness.
2. **Don't Rely on Your Own Understanding:** Our understanding is limited, but God's wisdom is infinite. We're reminded not to lean on our understanding but instead to rely on God's wisdom and guidance.
3. **Acknowledge God in All Your Ways:** God's guidance isn't just for life's big decisions. We are to acknowledge Him in all our ways – in every decision, every situation, every moment. We are

to seek His guidance and recognize His presence in every aspect of our lives.

4. **God Will Direct Your Paths**: When we trust God, lean not on our understanding, and acknowledge Him in all our ways, He promises to direct our paths. This means He will guide us in the right direction according to His perfect plan and purpose for our lives.

CONCLUSION:

Proverbs 3:5-6 gently reminds us that life isn't about figuring out everything ourselves. Instead, it encourages us to lean on God's understanding, wisdom, timing, and perfect plan. Trusting God means more than just acknowledging His existence. It means relying on Him in every aspect of our lives, from the most significant decisions to the most minor details.

The verses emphasize active listening for God's voice in solitude and in the middle of our everyday lives. It's about making God a part of our daily routines, decision-making processes, and reflections. The passage assures us that when we truly learn to trust God and listen for His guidance, He will lead us along the right path, ensuring we stay on track. According to these verses, trusting God is the blueprint for a secure and fulfilled life.

REFLECTION:

1. Reflect on your current level of trust in God. How can you grow in your faith to trust Him 'from the bottom of your heart'? What steps can you take toward increasing this trust, even when situations are challenging or uncertain?
2. Consider a recent decision or situation where you relied on your understanding. How might the outcome have differed if you had sought God's guidance?
3. What does it mean to you to 'listen for God's voice in everything you do'? Can you recall a time when you experienced this?
4. How can you practice being more attentive to God's voice in your day-to-day life? What are certain habits or routines you could develop to help with this?
5. Reflect on the phrase, 'He's the one who will keep you on track.' How does that resonate with your personal experiences or your faith journey?

PRAYER:

Dear God, I come before You today with a humble and open heart. I seek to deepen my trust in You, embracing the wisdom of leaning not on my understanding but on Your divine guidance. Help me recognize that my knowledge and intuition, while valuable, are limited without Your divine perspective.

In the quiet moments and in the chaos, help me listen for Your voice. Guide me to be more aware of Your presence in everything I do and everywhere I go. Let me not simply hear but also understand and act upon Your guidance.

When I feel lost or uncertain, remind me that You are there to keep me on track, and to guide my steps according to Your will. I pray that my faith in You grows stronger daily, anchoring me amidst life's storms and guiding me on clear days.

Thank you for your unfailing love and guidance that light up my path. I place my trust in You, today and always.

In Jesus' name, I pray. Amen.

GOING DEEPER:

Reflect on what you have read and prayed for and take a moment to personalize your insights.

1. Think about what it means to you when you say, 'I trust God from the bottom of my heart.' How does this trust shape what you expect from God, the way you act and how you pray? If a friend was having difficulty trusting God, what would you tell them about how you learned to trust Him more deeply?
2. 'Listening for God's voice in everything you do' can sometimes mean making choices that don't align with what others expect of you. Can you think of a situation where you might need to make such a choice? How can you prepare yourself to stay true to God's guidance in such cases?
3. Imagine your life five years from now, having fully embraced the practice of trusting God 'from the bottom of your heart.' What changes do you foresee in your attitudes, choices and relationships?
4. How can you encourage others around you to trust in God more and pay attention to what He might be telling them?

NAVIGATING YOUR JOURNEY:

When reflecting on how to cultivate a lifestyle of seeking and acknowledging God's guidance, here are a few suggestions:

1. Set aside a few quiet moments daily to listen for God's voice. This could be early in the morning, during a lunch break or before bedtime. Use this time for prayer, reflection, or simply to be still in God's presence.

2. Start a 'Trust Journal.' Each day, write down one instance where you trusted in God or sought His guidance. This can help you become more aware of how often you lean on God.

3. Share your goal of trusting God more with a trusted friend or family member. They can help you stay focused on your journey, offer encouragement and share their experiences of trusting God.

4. At the end of each week, take some time to reflect on your progress. Celebrate success, no matter how small, and consider areas where you can further grow your trust in God.

Remember that seeking God's guidance is a journey. Be patient with yourself and be open to His leading, even when it doesn't align with your own understanding.

Day 14: Praise: A Heartfelt Anthem to the Lord

FOCUS:

Gratitude

SONG:

Blessings - Lecrae

INTRODUCTION:

PSALM 103, A BEAUTIFUL hymn of David, is filled with gratitude and praise for God's endless love, mercy, and blessings. The Psalm serves as a reminder, encouraging us not to forget all God's benefits. It calls us to remember His forgiveness, healing, redemption, compassion, and unchanging love. As we navigate the challenges and triumphs of life, it is essential that we keep this perspective of gratitude, recognizing and acknowledging God's goodness in all situations.

READING:

Psalm 103 (NLT)

Let all that I am praise the Lord; with my whole heart, I will praise his holy name. Let all that I am praise the Lord; may I never forget the good things he does for me. He forgives all my sins and heals all my diseases. He redeems me from death and crowns me with love and tender mercies. He fills my life with good things. My youth is renewed like the eagle's!

The Lord gives righteousness and justice to all who are treated unfairly. He revealed his character to Moses and his deeds to the people of Israel. The Lord is compassionate and merciful, slow to get angry and filled with unfailing love. He will not constantly accuse us, nor remain angry forever. He does not punish us for all our sins; he does not deal harshly with us, as we deserve. For his unfailing love toward those who fear him is as great as the height of the heavens above the earth. He has removed our sins as far from us as the east is from the west.

The Lord is like a father to his children, tender and compassionate to those who fear him. For he knows how weak we are; he remembers we are only dust. Our days on earth are like grass; like wildflowers, we bloom and die. The wind blows, and we are gone — as though we had never been here. But the love of the Lord remains forever with those who fear him. His salvation extends to the children's children of those who are faithful to his covenant, of those who obey his commandments!

The Lord has made the heavens his throne; from there he rules over everything. Praise the Lord, you angels, you mighty ones who carry out his plans, listening for each of his commands. Yes, praise the Lord, you armies of angels who serve him and do his will! Praise the Lord, everything he has created, everything in all his kingdom. Let all that I am praise the Lord.

KEY PRINCIPLES:

1. **Praise God Wholeheartedly:** Our gratitude and praise should encompass all our being. It is not just about uttering words of thanksgiving but letting our whole life—our actions, attitudes, and thoughts—reflect our praise to God.
2. **Never Forget His Benefits:** It's easy to forget God's goodness, especially when we face hardships. However, David reminds us to remember God's blessings—Forgiveness, healing, redemption, and love.
3. **Embrace God's Love and Mercy:** God's love and mercy are not earned but given freely. Understanding this truth should lead us to a place of deep gratitude and love for God.

CONCLUSION:

As we digest the heartfelt sentiments of Psalm 103, we're presented with an image of God's unwavering love and kindness. This isn't just an urge to be thankful but a nudge toward a deeper, more meaningful relationship with Him, built on love, mercy and a constant acknowledgment of His benevolent gifts in our lives.

This Psalm reminds us that God's compassion is greater than our human flaws, providing us with healing and forgiveness. Our lives on earth may be short, like wildflowers that bloom and fade, but God's love is everlasting, wrapping us and generations to come in its warm embrace.

It implores us to live our lives appreciating God's goodness and mercy, regardless of our situations. As we continue our spiritual journey, let's strive to demonstrate God's love in our actions, continually praising Him for His enduring affection.

REFLECTION:

1. Reflect on your practice of gratitude. How can you cultivate a deeper sense of appreciation that

is rooted in remembering God's benefits?

2. Consider your praise life. What does it mean for you to "praise God with all that you are"? How can you integrate praise more fully into your daily routines and interactions?

3. In what situations do you find it challenging to remember God's benefits? How can you shift your perspective to recognize God's love and mercy in these circumstances?

4. How can you align your life more closely with the teachings of Psalm 103? What practical steps can you take to embrace gratitude and praise more fully?

5. Which verse or part of the Psalm resonated with you the most? Why did it stand out, and what significance does it hold for your life and faith journey?

PRAYER:

Dear God, I come before you today, recognizing Your infinite love and mercy. Whether in times of joy or moments of despair, I am grateful for Your unfailing presence. I acknowledge Your gifts of forgiveness, healing, redemption and tender mercies that are always within reach, even when they may seem distant.

In the moments when I may feel empty or forgotten, please give me the strength to see Your blessings and mercy during my struggles. Guide me to find hope and reassurance in Your promise that Your love for me is unchanging and everlasting.

Help me, dear Lord, to offer my wholehearted praise to You, allowing my life to reflect my deep gratitude. As I strive to embrace and live the teachings of Psalm 103, I hope to experience Your love and mercy in new and comforting ways.

May Your enduring love not only touch my life but also bring comfort and joy to those who feel they are in the shadows. Please illuminate their paths with Your grace, mercy and love.

In Jesus' name, I pray. Amen.

GOING DEEPER:

1. Psalm 103 speaks to God's character as merciful, forgiving and righteous. How can this image of God shape your understanding of His role in our life? How does it challenge or reinforce your existing beliefs?

2. The Psalmist uses vivid imagery to convey the briefness of human life and the enduring nature of God's love. How does this comparison affect your view of earthly worries or challenges? How does it influence your priorities or values?

3. Reflect on the phrase "as far as the east is from the west" used in the Psalm to describe God's forgiveness. What does this metaphor mean to you personally? How does it shape your understanding of God's mercy?

4. The Psalm highlights God's kindness toward those who honor His covenant and obey His commandments. How does this affect your interpretation of faithfulness? What steps can you take to express your faithfulness to God more clearly?

5. David frequently acknowledges and praises God's acts of mercy and kindness in this Psalm. How can you incorporate the act of recognizing God's mercy in your life more consciously? How might this affect your relationship with God and others?

NAVIGATING YOUR JOURNEY:

To personalize the lesson and reflect on how to cultivate a lifestyle of gratitude and praise, consider these suggestions:

1. Find a verse or phrase from Psalm 103 that particularly resonates with you and make it your daily reminder. Write it on a Post-it note, set it as your phone wallpaper or place it where you'll see it often to remind you of God's enduring love and mercy.

2. Incorporate praise breaks into your daily routine. These could be short moments throughout the day where you pause to praise God for His goodness. This could be done through singing, prayer, or simply acknowledging His presence.

3. In challenging situations, make an effort to seek God's mercy. Try to shift your perspective and look for signs of His love and compassion even in difficult circumstances.

4. Reflect on how you can extend God's enduring love and kindness to others in your life. This could be through acts of kindness, offering help, or simply being there for someone in need. By doing so, you're not just experiencing God's love but also becoming a channel of His love to others.

Day 15: Wisdom's Path: Insight for a Purposeful Life

FOCUS:

Wisdom

SONG:

God in Me – Mary Mary

INTRODUCTION:

IN PROVERBS 16:16-33, we are encouraged to deeply examine the values we hold dear and the paths we choose to follow. The verses offer rich wisdom about the significance of insight over wealth. As we journey through these verses, prepare to gain invaluable understanding regarding the consequences of decisions and the power of leading a life guided by wisdom and self-control.

READING:

Proverbs 16:16-33 (MSG)

Get wisdom—it's worth more than money; choose insight over income every time. The road of right living bypasses evil; watch your step and save your life. First pride, then the crash—the bigger the ego, the harder the fall. It's better to live humbly among the poor than to live it up among the rich and famous. It pays to take life seriously; things work out when you trust in God.

A wise person gets known for insight; gracious words add to one's reputation. True intelligence is a spring of fresh water, while fools sweat it out the hard way. They make a lot of sense, these wise folks; whenever they speak, their reputation increases.

Gracious speech is like clover honey – good taste to the soul, quick energy for the body.

There's a way that looks harmless enough; look again—it leads straight to hell. Appetite is an incentive to work; hunger makes you work all the harder.

Mean people spread mean gossip; their words smart and burn. Troublemakers start fights; gossip breaks up friendships. Calloused climbers betray their very own friends; they stab their own grandmothers in the back. A shifty eye betrays an evil intention; a clenched jaw signals trouble ahead.

Gray hair is a mark of distinction, the award for a God-loyal life. Moderation is better than muscle, self-control better than political power. Make your motions and cast your votes, but God has the final say.

KEY PRINCIPLES:

1. **Value of Wisdom:** The scripture elevates wisdom above wealth, emphasizing its vital role in guiding us toward right living.
2. **Warning Against Pride:** The passage warns us that pride often leads to a fall. It encourages humility and living simply among the less privileged instead of seeking fame and riches.
3. **Power of Gracious Speech:** Words spoken wisely and kindly can nourish our souls like honey and energize our bodies.
4. **Consequences of Mean Gossip:** The passage warns about the destructive power of harmful gossip, reminding us of the importance of being mindful of our words.
5. **Importance of Moderation and Self-control:** The scripture praises moderation and self-control, emphasizing their superiority over brute strength or political power.

CONCLUSION:

Proverbs 16:16-33 presents insights and practical wisdom that urges us to look beyond material wealth and superficial success. It illuminates the path of wisdom, a way marked not by the glitter of gold or the allure of fame but by humility, kindness and self-control.

These verses compel us to reflect on the nature of pride and its inevitable downfall. They emphasize the power and significance of our words, advocating for gracious speech. Coupled with moderation and self-control, the wisdom shared in these verses encourages us to make thoughtful, wise choices, not just for the benefit of ourselves but also for the harmony of our communities.

REFLECTION:

1. The scripture warns against the destructive consequences of pride. Have there been instances in your life where pride has led to a fall? How did you learn from this experience?
2. Reflect on the power of gracious speech. Can you recall a time when kind words positively impacted you or someone else? How did it make you feel? Can you identify situations where you can apply more gracious speech in your daily life?

3. We are cautioned against mean gossip. Have you ever been involved in spreading or receiving gossip? What were the consequences, and what have you learned from that experience?

4. Take a moment to identify areas of your life where you need to practice more self-control. What steps can you take toward this? How do you ensure you don't take the idea of self-control too far and go overboard?

5. We learned that God has the final say. Do you surrender control to God, believing that He will guide you to the right path, or do you often feel the need to control the outcome yourself?

6. Proverbs suggest that true intelligence is like a refreshing water spring, while foolishness leads to unnecessary hard work. Can you recall an instance where wisdom made your life easier? Or a situation where a lack of wisdom led to extra difficulties?

PRAYER:

Dear Heavenly Father, in a world where wealth and power often take center stage, guide me to value wisdom and insight above all else. Fill my heart with the humility to acknowledge my imperfections and the eagerness to learn from my mistakes. Let my words be kind and gracious, radiating Your love and peace to those around me.

Please help me to recognize and avoid the pitfalls of pride and instead lead me down the path of righteousness. Teach me the strength that lies in moderation and self-control so that I may reflect these virtues in my daily life. Let me remember that a life guided by wisdom is the true path to happiness and fulfillment.

Lord, guard my heart against the harm of idle gossip and instill in me the spirit of unity and brotherhood/sisterhood. Help me to honor the mark of distinction You've placed upon me as I grow older, to live out my years in loyalty and faithfulness to You.

Thank You for the wisdom You've imparted through Your Word. As I continue my journey, may I embody these principles in my actions and decisions.

In Jesus' name, I pray. Amen.

GOING DEEPER:

1. Wisdom is esteemed in the scripture above material wealth. However, society often glorifies wealth and fame. How do you balance these contrasting views in your daily life and decision-making processes? How does your faith guide you in this?

2. Pride is identified as a stumbling block in the scripture. Can you identify subtle ways in which

pride manifests in your daily life? What proactive steps can you take to counteract these tendencies?

3. Gracious speech is likened to honey, nourishing to the body and soul. Are there people in your life you need to engage more graciously with? What measures can you take to ensure your words reflect grace and wisdom?

4. We talked earlier about the importance of moderation and self-control. Are there areas of your life where excess has become a problem? How can you practice moderation in these areas without veering into legalism or extreme denial?

5. The destructive power of gossip is highlighted in the scripture. Have you noticed patterns or environments where you are more susceptible to engaging in gossip? How can you confront and change these patterns?

6. Reflect on the metaphor of true intelligence being like a spring of fresh water and foolishness leading to hard labor. Are there areas of your life where you could apply more wisdom to make your work and life more refreshing and less strenuous? What are the steps you could take toward achieving this?

7. The passage reminds us that God has the final say. Can you identify times when you've tried to take control from God? What were the results? Dig deeper and try to understand why you were reluctant to relinquish control. Were there specific fears or concerns that held you back? How can you work toward surrendering these fears or your desires and plans to His will and wisdom in the future?

NAVIGATING YOUR JOURNEY:

1. Pursue wisdom, not wealth. Remember, wisdom is more valuable than wealth. Make learning and understanding a priority in your life. Engage in activities that improve your knowledge and insight. Read widely, ask questions and seek to understand different perspectives.

2. Cultivate humility. Keep your ego in check. Recognize the contributions and worth of others, and don't let pride lead you astray. Share your achievements with humility, and always remember where you come from.

3. Speak graciously to others and yourself. Be mindful of the words you speak, both to others and yourself. Strive to use kind, encouraging words that build others up and don't forget to show the same kindness to yourself. Speak affirmations and positivity into your life. Avoid gossip, hurtful language and self-deprecating talk. Remember, how we talk to ourselves often shapes our self-perception and interactions with the world.

4. Practice moderation and self-control. Develop discipline in your daily life. This could be in your diet, work habits, spending or reactions to others. Moderation is about maintaining

balance, not excess. Self-control is about managing our actions and reactions effectively rather than trying to control or dominate others aggressively.

5. Let go and let God. Understand that not everything is within your control, and that's okay. Remember, once you surrender a situation to God, try not to take back control by worrying about it or trying to manage it yourself. It's challenging to let go of control, especially when we're afraid. It's natural to feel reluctant or fearful. When fear creeps in, remind yourself of God's omnipotence and love for you. Talk to Him about your worries and ask for His peace and courage. As you practice this, trusting in His wisdom and guidance becomes easier.

6. Practice reflection. Regularly take time for self-reflection. This practice helps you stay aware of your actions and your decisions...and the effect of both. It encourages personal growth and the development of wisdom.

Keep in mind that wisdom and self-control are not achieved overnight but gradually as you navigate the winding path of life. Celebrate every victory, every insight gained and every moment of growth. Each step you take, no matter how small, is a testament to your progress and a step closer to living in alignment with God's wisdom. As you move forward, remember that even the stumbles and setbacks are opportunities to grow, learn, and gain deeper insight into God's plan for you. So, keep going, keep growing and keep seeking wisdom in every step of your journey.

Day 16: In the Presence of a Shepherd

FOCUS:

Guidance

SONG:

God Only Knows - For King & Country

INTRODUCTION:

PSALM 23, PENNED BY King David, offers us an image of God as a shepherd who provides, guides and protects. David's confidence in God's guidance is not based on his own understanding or strength but stems from a deep trust in God's love and faithfulness. This Psalm is a powerful reminder that when we surrender our paths to God, He leads us in the right direction, even through the darkest valleys.

READING:

Psalm 23 (NLT)

The Lord is my shepherd; I have all that I need. He lets me rest in green meadows; he leads me beside peaceful streams. He renews my strength. He guides me along right paths, bringing honor to his name. Even when I walk through the darkest valley, I will not be afraid, for you are close beside me. Your rod and your staff protect and comfort me. You prepare a feast for me in the presence of my enemies. You honor me by anointing my head with oil. My cup overflows with blessings. Surely your goodness and unfailing love will pursue me all the days of my life, and I will live in the house of the Lord forever.

KEY PRINCIPLES:

1. **God as a Providing Shepherd:** The psalm begins with the metaphor of the Lord as a shepherd, signifying His role as a provider and caretaker. Like a shepherd caring for his sheep, God meets our needs, offers rest and brings renewal.

2. **Guidance and Protection:** The psalmist, King David, emphasizes God's guidance along the right paths and His protection, even in the most challenging circumstances. God's rod and staff

symbolize His power to protect and authority to guide us.

3. **God's Presence and Comfort:** David highlights God's comforting presence in the face of fear and adversity. Despite waking through the darkest valleys, he finds comfort in knowing God is by his side.

4. **God's Favor and Blessings:** The psalm depicts God's favor as a feast prepared even in the presence of enemies, signifying His overflowing blessings, honor and provision.

5. **Assurance of God's Goodness and Love:** The psalm concludes with a confident assurance of God's goodness and love that follows us throughout our lives. And it ends with a statement of faith in a perpetual dwelling in the house of the Lord.

6. **Trust in God:** The overall tone of this psalm demonstrates a deep, unwavering trust in God's faithfulness and His capacity to guide, protect and provide. It reminds us to surrender our paths to God and trust His guidance...even through the darkest valleys.

CONCLUSION:

Psalm illustrates a profound trust in God's guidance and protection, painting a vivid image of God as our Shepherd who lovingly provides for our needs, guides us along the right paths and stands by our side even in our darkest moments. This Psalm prompts us to deeply consider our own relationship with God and emphasizes the importance of surrendering control to Him and trusting in His unwavering love and goodness. As we navigate life's challenges, the wisdom encapsulated in these verses serves as a reminder not to be governed by fear or uncertainty but to allow God's comforting presence and provision to overflow in our lives, affirming that His unfailing love will follow us all our days.

REFLECTION:

1. Think about God as a Shepherd. How have you personally experienced God's guidance, provision and protection?

2. David expresses a deep trust in God, even in the darkest valleys. Can you recall when you had to lean into your faith during a difficult period? What did you learn from that experience?

3. Recognizing God's constant presence and care, as portrayed in today's lesson, can bring a profound sense of comfort and security. In moments when you face challenges or difficulties, how does this image of God shape your feelings, reactions and decisions?

4. In what ways do you see God's "goodness and unfailing love" pursuing you in your day-to-day life? Can you identify specific instances where you felt God's love in action?

5. The Psalm concludes with the confident statement of 'living in the house of the Lord forever.'

How does this promise stir your heart? What feelings does it arouse within you knowing this is possible?

PRAYER:

DEAR GOD, YOU ARE MY Shepherd, my Provider and my Protector. My heart is filled with gratitude for the abundant blessings You shower upon me – blessings I received in the past, those I am walking in now, and those that You will provide in my future. Forgive me for when I neglected to appreciate You and your guidance, provision and protection as I should have.

Father, even when fear grips me, when I find myself in the darkest valleys of life, You infuse me with courage. My faith in Your constant protection and guidance propels me forward.

You remind me, Lord, that I lack nothing in Your presence. You renew my strength and guide me along the right paths. The promise of dwelling in Your house forever fills me with an overwhelming sense of peace and comfort.

I pray, Lord, for the grace to surrender myself more fully to You, trust in Your wisdom, and accept Your endless love and goodness. Guide me as I navigate through life, holding steadfast to the belief that Your goodness and love will follow me all the days of my life.

In Jesus' name, I pray. Amen.

GOING DEEPER:

1. The Psalmist expresses that God's 'goodness and unfailing love' actively pursues us. Reflect on this idea of being pursued by God's love. How does it make you feel to know that God's love is not passive but actively seeks you out, especially in moments when you might feel undeserving or distant? Can you identify instances in your life where you have felt this active pursuit of God's love?
2. King David composed this Psalm from a place of intimate relationship and trust in God. Are there any obstacles you face in fully trusting God as your Shepherd? How can you overcome these barriers?
3. The Psalm offers a beautiful image of God preparing a feast for us in the presence of our enemies. How does this perspective challenge how you view your adversities and God's role in them?
4. The Psalm speaks of God guiding us along 'right paths.' Think about a time when God's path for you seemed unclear or uncertain. How did you navigate this? What can this teach you

about God's guidance in the future?

5. Reflect on your self-perception. Are there instances where feelings of unworthiness or imposter syndrome have hindered you from recognizing or accepting God's blessings and provisions? How can you align your self-perceptions with God's unconditional love for you?

6. God's love for us is not dependent on our merit or worthiness. However, we often find it hard to grasp this truth fully. What practical steps can you take to remind yourself of God's unconditional love and grace, especially when feelings of unworthiness creep in?

7. In the scripture, David uses the metaphor of God as a shepherd and us as His sheep. Some people may interpret this metaphor as suggesting passivity or blind obedience. However, in the biblical context, it conveys God's care, guidance and protection. How does this understanding influence your perspective on this metaphor? What does it tell you about your relationship with God?

NAVIGATING YOUR JOURNEY:

1. Embrace God's presence. Make time for quiet reflection or meditation each day to feel God's presence. Whether through prayer, reading scriptures or just sitting in silence, acknowledge His comforting presence and let it bring you peace.

2. Active trust in God. Trust is an active verb. It requires decision and action. In times of uncertainty or challenge, remember to consciously choose to trust in God's guidance and protection.

3. Affirmations of God's love. Positive affirmations can be a powerful way to remind yourself of God's love and provision. Consider using phrases like "God's love and goodness are pursuing me or "The Lord is my shepherd; I lack nothing" as daily reminders.

4. Acknowledge your worth. Remember, God's love for you is unconditional and does not depend on your achievements, failures or how deserving you feel. When feelings of unworthiness creep in, remind yourself of God's endless love for you.

5. View challenges as opportunities. The Psalmist writes about a feast prepared in the presence of enemies. Try to see challenges as opportunities for growth and envision how God might be using these situations to prepare a 'feast' for you.

6. Keep a gratitude journal. Start a practice of noting down instances where you felt God's love, care and provision in your day-to-day life. Over time, this can help you recognize and appreciate God's constant presence and guidance.

7. Reevaluate the Shepherd and Sheep Metaphor. Spend time reevaluating the metaphor of being a sheep under God's shepherdship. As you ponder this, remember that this image does not convey mindless obedience but rather a relationship of trust, care and guidance.

8. Open your heart to be pursued. Reflect on how it feels to be pursued by God's love and allow your heart to be open to this active, persistent love. God's love seeks to comfort, heal and draw you closer to Him—allow yourself to be pursued. It's essential to remember that God's love is not like human love, which can sometimes be selfish, inconsistent, stingy or abusive. His love is constant, unconditional, and not based on merit or performance. Always remember that God's love is pure and unchanging, so don't compare His love and pursuit with any other form of love you may have experienced.

The journey of faith is an ongoing process, filled with highs and lows, moments of clarity and confusion. Through all of this, remember that you are not alone—God, your Shepherd, is with you every step of the way. He guides you, protects you and provides for you. He pursues you with His unwavering love. Understand that His love is not like human love—it is constant, unconditional and unchanging. As you navigate your journey, keep in mind these practical steps. Whether you are reconnecting with the Shepherd, trusting in His paths, confronting your fears or opening your heart to be pursued by His love, remember always to be patient with yourself. Your spiritual journey is your own; taking it at your own pace is okay.

Day 17: A Song of Thankfulness and Trust

FOCUS:

Gratitude

SONG:

You Know My Name – Tasha Cobbs Leonard

INTRODUCTION:

PSALM 138 IS A HEARTFELT hymn of gratitude. David, amidst all his struggles, always found reasons to thank God. His deep trust in God's unfailing love and faithfulness is a profound reminder for us to cultivate a similar attitude of gratitude in our lives.

READING:

Psalm 138 (MSG)

Thank you! Everything in me says 'Thank you!' Angels listen as I sing my thanks. I kneel in worship facing your holy temple and say it again: 'Thank you!' Thank you for your love, thank you for your faithfulness; Most holy is your name, most holy is your Word. The moment I called out, you stepped in; you made my life large with strength. When they hear what you have to say, God, all earth's kings will say 'Thank you.' They'll sing of what you've done: 'How great the glory of God!' And here's why: God, high above, sees far below; no matter the distance, he knows everything about us. When I walk into the thick of trouble, keep me alive in the angry turmoil. With one hand strike my foes, With your other hand save me. Finish what you started in me, God. Your love is eternal—don't quit on me now.

KEY PRINCIPLES:

1. **Thank God with All Your Heart:** David expresses his gratitude to God with his whole being. This genuine, heartfelt thankfulness is a model for us to emulate in our own expressions of appreciation.

2. **God's Love and Faithfulness:** We see the depth of David's gratitude stemming from his

understanding of God's love and faithfulness. As we grow in our knowledge of these divine attributes, our own gratitude should deepen.

3. **God's Response to Our Call:** The psalmist reminds us that God steps in when we call out to Him. Remembering and thanking God for His past interventions helps us to trust Him for the future.

4. **God's Omniscience:** God's intimate knowledge of our lives is another reason for our gratitude. Despite the distance or our circumstances, God knows us thoroughly and cares for our needs.

5. **God's Protection and Salvation:** David trusts in God's protection and salvation even during trouble. Gratitude in the face of trials is a powerful act of faith, acknowledging that God is at work even in our difficulties.

6. **God's Unfinished Work and Eternal Love:** David acknowledges that God is still at work in his life. His confidence in God's eternal love and ongoing work is a call for us also to thank God for His continuing work in our lives.

CONCLUSION:

Psalm 138 is a beautiful reminder of God's love, faithfulness and presence in our lives. It encourages us to be grateful even during trials and challenges. It prompts us to thank God wholeheartedly for His intimate knowledge of us, His timely interventions and His ongoing work in our lives. As we move forward, let us strive to express gratitude in all circumstances, trusting in God's love and faithfulness. This act of thankfulness is not just about acknowledging the good times but also recognizing God's guiding hand in our challenges and difficult seasons. Let's invite God into our journey, allowing Him to complete the work He has started in us as we continue to trust in His eternal love.

REFLECTION:

1. How does David's expression of gratitude to God in this Psalm inspire or challenge you in your expressions of thankfulness?

2. David thanks God for His love and faithfulness. Reflect on moments when you've personally experienced God's love and faithfulness. How does this deepen your sense of gratitude?

3. The Psalm highlights God's immediate response when we call out to Him. Can you recall instances where you've experienced God stepping in during times of need? How did this impact your trust in Him?

4. David is aware of God's intimate knowledge of his life. How does the idea that God knows everything about you and cares for your needs influence your relationship with Him? Does this knowledge prompt gratitude?

5. Even in trouble, David trusts God's protection and salvation. Have there been difficult moments in your life where you've seen God's protecting hand? How did these experiences shape your faith and gratitude?
6. David acknowledges that God's work in him is ongoing. In what areas of your life do you see God's ongoing work? How does this inspire you to be grateful and trusting of His eternal love?

PRAYER:

Dear God, from the deepest corners of my heart, I want to say, 'Thank You.' You have shown me love and faithfulness beyond measure, and I am forever grateful for that. Every breath I take and every moment I live is a testament to Your goodness.

I am in awe of Your omniscience, the way You see me, know me and understand me completely. Even when I'm far off or lost in life's challenges, Your care for me is unchanging. Lord, I offer my deepest thanks for Your intimate knowledge of my life.

When I walk through trials, You're my sanctuary, my shelter, my protection and my strength. I have seen Your hand of protection and salvation in my life, even in the most challenging times. In the face of turmoil, I choose to trust in You and express my gratitude, for You are always at work, even when I fail to see it.

I am confident that You are not done with me yet, Lord. Your love is eternal, and Your work in me is ongoing. For all the ways You've shaped me and all the ways You will continue to shape me, I say 'Thank you.'

Help me cultivate a heart of gratitude every day, Lord, not just for the blessings I can see but also for the unseen works of Your hand. Thank You for Your faithfulness today and always.

In Jesus' name, I pray. Amen.

GOING DEEPER:

Take a moment to personalize and reflect on what you have read and prayed:

1. Consider the phrase, "God, high above, sees far below; no matter the distance, he knows everything about us." This idea of God's omniscience, or all-knowing nature, can sometimes seem to conflict with the notion of free will. How do you reconcile these two concepts in your personal faith journey? Do you see God's knowledge of you as a limitation on your freedom or a testament to His deep care and understanding? Reflect on how God's complete knowledge of

you could potentially deepen your relationship with Him, knowing that He fully understands you yet gives you the freedom to choose your actions.

2. Reflect on the phrase, "Finish what you started in me, God. Your love is eternal—don't quit on me now." David expresses trust in God's ongoing work within him. In your own life, can you identify areas where you believe God began a work in you, but progress seems to have halted? These areas can be related to your personal, professional, emotional or spiritual life. Consider whether there might be any actions, habits or attitudes within you that might be impeding the process. How can you collaborate with God to rekindle this work and allow His transformative love to manifest in those areas of your life fully?

3. Think about your current environment – the places you frequent and the people you interact with regularly. How are these impacting the different areas of your life where you believe God has started a work in you? Are there any situations or relationships that feel like "infertile or poisoned soil," hindering the progress and growth in your personal, professional, emotional or spiritual life? How might you alter your environment or manage these relationships to create a more nurturing context for your growth? This might involve setting boundaries, seeking new relationships/friendships or even changing physical locations. How can you collaborate with God in this progress to cultivate fertile soil for your growth and transformation in all areas of your life?

4. The Psalmist expresses faith in God's faithfulness and love, and these attributes are what inspire his gratitude. How have you personally experienced God's faithfulness and love in your life? Are there instances where you've found it hard to perceive His faithfulness and love? Reflect on these experiences and how they've shaped your understanding of God and your relationship with Him.

5. The passage states, "All the earth's kings will say 'Thank you' when they hear what God has to say." This verse suggests the universal reach and impact of God's Word. How can you contribute to sharing God's message of love and faithfulness in your life? Remember, you don't have to be a formal minister or evangelist to do this – every interaction, every act of kindness, every moment of integrity can be a powerful testimony. How might your daily choices, actions or words reflect God's love and faithfulness within your sphere of influence, no matter how big or small? Think about the ripple effect of your influence in spreading God's message.

NAVIGATING YOUR JOURNEY:

1. Express gratitude. Cultivate a habit of expressing gratitude to God daily. It doesn't have to be

an elaborate prayer, just a simple 'Thank You' for His love, faithfulness and continued work in your life.

2. Embrace God's omnipresence. God knows everything about you, and this should not be seen as a limitation but instead as an assurance of His deep care and understanding. Remind yourself of His intimate knowledge and let this deepen your trust and dependence on Him.

3. Acknowledge God's work in your life. Reflect regularly on the areas of your life where God has begun a work. This could be personal, professional, emotional or spiritual. If you feel the progress has halted, try to identify what actions or habits could be hindering this and how you can collaborate with God to resume this transformative process.

4. Evaluate your environment. Consider whether the places and people you regularly interact with nourish or hinder your growth. You might need to make some changes, set some boundaries or seek new relationships that align more closely with your growth journey. Understand that others may not always perceive your changes in a positive light and might even accuse you of being selfish or acting superior. However, remember that wanting to improve, grow and align more closely with the work God is doing in your life is not a selfish act or an attempt to elevate yourself above others. It's about creating a nurturing environment that supports your growth and progression.

5. Reflect God's love and faithfulness. In your day-to-day life, consciously make an effort to reflect God's love and faithfulness. Your words, actions and even attitudes can be a powerful testimony. You do not need to be a pastor to spread God's message; simply live it out in your life.

6. Trust in His eternal love and unfinished work. Maintain a deep-seated belief that God's love for you is eternal, and He is not finished with you yet. His work in you is ongoing, and His love is unwavering. Trust Him and remember that He won't quit on you now.

IN NAVIGATING OUR JOURNEY, it's essential to remember that the path to personal growth and transformation is multifaceted, involving both introspection and outward actions. Above all, remember that this journey is not a solitary endeavor - it's a partnership with God, who is ever-present, infinitely loving and ceaselessly working in you.

Day 18: Wisdom in Action – Living Well and Building Community

---

FOCUS:

Wisdom

SONG:

If The Lord Builds The House – Hope Darst

INTRODUCTION:

James 3:13-18 challenges us to think about wisdom in a whole new way. These verses show us that being wise isn't just about being smart or talking a good game. It's about how we live our lives – how we treat others, how we handle our ambitions, and how we maintain consistency in our actions.

READING:

James 3:13-18 (MSG)

Do you want to be counted wise, to build a reputation for wisdom? Here's what you do: Live well, live wisely, live humbly. It's the way you live, not the way you talk, that counts. Mean-spirited ambition isn't wisdom. Boasting that you are wise isn't wisdom. Twisting the truth to make yourselves sound wise isn't wisdom. It's the furthest thing from wisdom — it's animal cunning, devilish conniving. Whenever you're trying to look better than others or get the better of others, things fall apart and everyone ends up at the others' throats. Real wisdom, God's wisdom, begins with a holy life and is characterized by getting along with others. It is gentle and reasonable, overflowing with mercy and blessings, not hot one day and cold the next, not two-faced. You can develop a healthy, robust community that lives right with God and enjoy its results only if you do the hard work of getting along with each other, treating each other with dignity and honor.

KEY PRINCIPLES:

1. **Living Wisely and Humbly:** According to James, the hallmark of true wisdom lies not in eloquent speech but in the quality of our lives. Wisdom manifests in how we live and treat others, emphasizing humility and a keen sense of understanding.

2. **Rejecting Mean-Spirited Ambition:** The text identifies mean-spirited ambition as contrary

to wisdom. It suggests that those who twist the truth or boast about their wisdom are not genuinely wise. Instead, such attitudes are likened to animal cunning and devilish conniving.

3. **Community Building Through Wisdom**: James emphasizes the crucial role of wisdom in fostering a robust community. This involves treating each other with dignity and honor, as well as hard work and cooperation. By adhering to these principles, individuals can contribute to a healthy, God-honoring community that lives in harmony and mutual respect. This wisdom-fueled community-building isn't just about individuals but about cultivating a collective relationship with God.

4. **Consistency in Character**: True wisdom is marked by consistency. It is "not hot one day and cold the next," implying that a truly wise person is not two-faced but remains consistent in their actions and attitudes.

5. **Gentleness, Reason and Mercy**: These are the characteristics of God's wisdom. James notes that wisdom is gentle and reasonable, "overflowing with mercy and blessings." This kind of wisdom aims for peace and understanding, promoting a positive and supportive community.

6. **Godly Wisdom vs. Worldly Wisdom**: James distinguishes between God's wisdom and the world's understanding of wisdom. God's wisdom begins with a holy life and is characterized by getting along with others, while worldly wisdom may involve selfish ambition and false appearances.

CONCLUSION:

James 3:13-18 invites us to step beyond the conventional understanding of wisdom as mere intellect or eloquence—it's a way of life marked by humility, gentleness and consistency. As we reflect on this powerful message, we are encouraged to soul-search and examine where our wisdom stems from – is it guided by the worldly standards of success and self-interest, or does it reflect divine wisdom characterized by humility, cooperation and consistency? True wisdom isn't simply knowing or speaking—it's about living and doing, rooted in divine teaching.

REFLECTION:

1. How does the idea that wisdom is more about how you live than what you say align with your personal experiences? Can you recall instances where you've seen this principle in action?

2. James warns against mean-spirited ambition. Reflect on times when you may have prioritized personal ambitions over community well-being. What can you learn from these experiences?

3. Reflect on your contribution to community-building. Do your actions and attitudes promote harmony and respect, or are there areas where you could improve?

4. Think about your character consistency. Are you the same person in private as you are in

public? If not, what drives the discrepancy, and how can you address it?

5. Contemplate your behavior toward others. Do gentleness, reason and mercy characterize your interactions? How can you cultivate these qualities more in your life?

6. Distinguish between godly wisdom and worldly wisdom in your life. Which one seems to guide your decisions more? How can you align your actions more closely with godly wisdom?

PRAYER:

Dear Heavenly Father, I come before you today with a heart seeking wisdom, not as the world sees it, but as You have defined it in Your holy word. I understand now, Lord, that true wisdom is not just about eloquent words or intellectual prowess. It's about how I live my life, treat others, and embody humility, gentleness and consistency.

Help me, Father, to reject mean-spirited ambition, to build a robust community of love and respect, and to demonstrate consistency in my character. Help me to embody the gentleness, reason and mercy that You treasure in a wise person.

Lord, I confess that I often fall into the trap of worldly wisdom, seeking my own advantage and striving for success. Please guide me to align my life more closely with Your divine wisdom. Let my actions, words and heart reflect the wisdom that begins with a holy life and is characterized by getting along with others.

In your mercy, Lord, help me to live wisely and humbly. May my life benefit from Your wisdom and serve as a beacon of Your divine wisdom to others.

In Jesus' name, I pray. Amen.

GOING DEEPER:

1. James describes godly wisdom as being gentle, reasonable and overflowing with mercy and blessings. Reflect on the most challenging situations you have faced or may face - perhaps high-stress situations, confrontations or dealing with difficult individuals. How can you cultivate and maintain these qualities of godly wisdom, even when emotions are high, stakes are elevated, and the instinctive reason might be to give in to anger and react harshly instead of maintaining gentleness and reason?

2. Reflect on moments when you've felt compelled to change your behavior due to societal expectations, peer pressure, workplace culture or survival. Consider instances where these adaptations might be considered necessary or protective, such as code-switching in different

cultural or professional environments. Then, consider situations where such changes may compromise your authenticity or core values. How can you navigate these complex dynamics while maintaining integrity and consistency in your character?

3. If we consider wisdom as a lifestyle rather than an accumulation of knowledge, how might this shift in perspective change your long-term goals and aspirations? How do you imagine this would impact your daily routines or habits?

4. James warns against mean-spirited ambition, contrasting it with wisdom that is rooted in humility, service and love. Reflect on the driving forces behind your ambitions. Are there elements of personal gain or power that motivate you? If so, examine these motivations: Are they born out of positive intentions like self-improvement or contributing to society, or do they ever verge toward causing harm or imbalance? Envision your ambitions as profoundly intertwined with service, humility and love. How would that influence your actions and shape your perspective of success? Use this inward exploration to discover how harmonizing your ambitions with genuine wisdom - which is marked by service, humility and love - can lead to transformative changes in your actions and redefine your understanding of success.

5. As you navigate life, how can you become more perceptive to instances where earthly wisdom—often characterized by self-interest or superficial success— might be subtly taking the place of divine wisdom in your decision-making? What practical steps can you take to enhance your discernment between these two types of wisdom in your everyday actions and choices?

6. Think about how the wisdom talked about in James 3:13-18 could be used not just in your personal life but in the broader world - your society or even across the globe. What things in society could benefit from this kind of humility, gentleness and wisdom that focuses on community? How might your approach to societal issues or supporting causes that you believe in change if the principles in James 3:13-18 consistently guided them? What steps could you take to spread this kind of wisdom to these broader areas? As you reflect on these questions, try to understand your potential role in encouraging a wider cultural shift toward this wisdom and how it could positively impact the world around you.

NAVIGATING YOUR JOURNEY:

1. Practice active listening. As James outlines, wisdom isn't just about speaking well but about listening carefully. Practice active listening in your conversations. Pay close attention to what others say and show genuine interest in understanding their perspective.

2. Mindful response. Before responding to situations or individuals, especially challenging ones, take a moment to pause and reflect. Consider if your planned response aligns with the qualities

of godly wisdom. Remember that gentleness implies a soft, compassionate approach; reasonableness suggests a fair and open-minded stance, while mercy involves forgiveness and leniency even when it's hard. Does your response resonate with these qualities?

3. Self-reflection. Regularly spend time in self-reflection to assess whether your actions align with godly wisdom or worldly wisdom. Identify areas where you may need to make changes and take practical steps toward doing so.

4. Promote community. Strive to build a sense of community in your personal and professional life. This could be through acts of service, supporting others and fostering open and respectful dialogues.

5. Consistency is vital. Endeavor to maintain consistency in your character across different environments and situations. This might mean standing by your core values even when it's difficult or unpopular.

6. Embrace humility. In your ambitions and successes, remain humble. Remember that the drive for personal gain or power should not override the importance of service, humility and love.

7. Educate yourself. Learn more about different cultures, societal issues and global challenges. This broader understanding can help you apply godly wisdom more effectively on a wider scale.

8. Take small steps. Implementing such significant changes may seem overwhelming. Remember that it's okay to start small. Even small changes in your actions or mindset can make a big difference in aligning closer with godly wisdom.

9. Prayer and meditation. Regular prayer or meditation can be a powerful tool in your journey toward embodying godly wisdom. Seek divine guidance and strength as you navigate through these changes.

10. Remember the ultimate goal. As you journey toward a life characterized by godly wisdom, remember that the ultimate goal isn't to achieve personal success. The ultimate goal is to live a life of service, humility, love and consistency that reflects the wisdom outlined in James 3:13-18.

As you undertake this transformative journey, remember that embodying godly wisdom is a continuous process, not a one-time achievement. Foster an open heart and mind to learn, change and grow. In all things you do, strive to reflect love and humility. Consider others' needs as equally important as your own. Seek wisdom. Let these virtues guide your actions, becoming your beacon in the journey. As you progress, your actions, big and small, will contribute to a ripple effect, making a difference not just in your life but in the wider world, too.

Day 19: Spirit-Led Journey: Answering the Call to Preach the Good News

---

FOCUS:

Guidance

SONG:

The Prayer – Celine Dion and Andrea Bocelli

INTRODUCTION:

The passage from Acts 16:6-10 demonstrates Paul and his companions' commitment to seeking and following God's guidance during their second missionary journey. When the Holy Spirit prevented them from preaching in Asia and Bithynia, they didn't despair. Instead, they listened for God's direction, which led them to Macedonia. This instance reminds us of the need to continually seek God's guidance in our lives and be open to changes in our plans according to His will. Through their experience, we see how perceived obstacles become gateways to new opportunities when one is attuned to divine guidance.

READING:

Acts 16:6-10 (MSG)

They went to Phrygia, and then on through the region of Galatia. Their plan was to turn west into Asia province, but the Holy Spirit blocked that route. So they went to Mysia and tried to go north to Bithynia, but the Spirit of Jesus wouldn't let them go there either. Proceeding on through Mysia, they went down to the seaport Troas. That night Paul had a dream: A Macedonian stood on the far shore and called across the sea, 'Come over to Macedonia and help us!' The dream gave Paul his map. We went to work at once getting things ready to cross over to Macedonia. All the pieces had come together. We knew now for sure that God had called us to preach the Good News to the Europeans.

KEY PRINCIPLES:

1. **Divine Guidance May Alter Our Plans:** Paul and his companions were open to God's leading, even when it meant altering their plans. Similarly, we should be willing to adjust our course according to God's direction.
2. **God Guides in Different Ways:** God can guide us through the Holy Spirit, dreams, circumstances, or people. It's crucial to stay alert and open to His leading in whatever form it may come.
3. **God's Guidance is Purposeful:** God's guidance led Paul and his team to Macedonia, where they were needed. God's direction in our lives always aligns with His greater plan and purpose.
4. **Immediate Obedience is Key:** Upon receiving God's guidance, Paul and his companions immediately prepared to go to Macedonia. We should also act promptly when we discern God's leading.

CONCLUSION:

The narrative in Acts 16:6-10 provides an insightful picture of divine guidance in action, reminding us of God's ever-present hand steering the course of our lives. It emphasizes that, like Paul and his companions, we are called to remain sensitive to Go's leading, prepared for shifts in our journey and ready for immediate action. The story portrays that divine guidance often unfolds unexpectedly and might disrupt our well-laid plans.

This scripture inspires us to cultivate a mindset of dynamic faith, reminding us that we are not merely drifting aimlessly but are divinely guided voyagers on life's ocean, bearing the Good News to the shores where we are called. The story of Paul's Macedonian call is not just a historical event but a living testimony, inspiring us to surrender to God's navigation and become flexible and prompt participants in His divine plan.

REFLECTION:

1. Can you recall a moment when you felt that God was leading you in a different direction than you had planned? How did you respond, and what were the outcomes?
2. How do you perceive divine guidance in your life? Do you believe God communicates with you through dreams, circumstances or other people, as he did with Paul?
3. Consider the principle of immediate obedience depicted in the scripture. Can you identify areas in your life where you might need to act promptly upon discerning God's direction?
4. How open are you to changes in your plans if they align with God's will? Is there any area where you are resisting a shift in direction?
5. How do you usually seek God's guidance in your life? In what ways can you improve your attentiveness to His leading?
6. Reflect on the purposefulness of God's guidance in your life. Consider how God's guidance can have far-reaching implications beyond your immediate circumstances. Can you identify instances where His direction aligned with a greater plan or purpose, even if it wasn't immediately apparent to you, but significantly impacted someone else's life, a project or an event in the world?

PRAYER:

GRACIOUS FATHER, THANK You for the unerring guidance You provide me. You see the grand tapestry of Your plan when all I see are the threads. When my ambition and plans blind me, gently remind me of Your higher purpose. Help me embrace change and trust that Your will might lead me along unexpected paths, but these paths are always for good.

Increase my sensitivity to Your guidance, Lord. Whether You choose to communicate with me through dreams, people or circumstances, open my ears and heart to receive Your divine direction. Strengthen my faith that I may act promptly when I discern Your guiding hand.

Help me to remember that Your guidance is not limited to my immediate circumstance. Let me be open to how Your plan might extend beyond my own life, impacting the lives of others and serving Your grand design.

In the maze of life, when I can't see the next turn, remind me that You are the ultimate Navigator. I surrender my plans to You, confident that Your wisdom transcends my understanding.

In Jesus' name, I pray. Amen.

GOING DEEPER:

1. God's communication is not always clear-cut or direct. How do you deal with moments of ambiguity or uncertainty in discerning His guidance? How can these experiences deepen your trust in God and your understanding of His ways?

2. Beyond dreams, consider how you perceive God communicates His guidance to you. Can you recount instances where you felt divine direction through circumstances, intuition, the counsel of others or even through an unexpected event? How did these experiences shape your understanding of His presence in your life, and how did they impact your future decisions or actions?

3. Dreams played a pivotal role in guiding Paul's journey in this passage. Have you ever experienced a dream that you felt contained guidance from the Lord? How did you interpret and respond to the dream? Did you believe it or dismiss the dream? Why?

4. Why do you think God blocks specific paths in our lives? What are the possible reasons behind God's redirection and the potential growth that might come from it?

5. Consider the notion that a closed door or a blocked route could be a form of holy protection or a redirection toward a greater purpose. Can you identify situations in your life where this might have been the case? How did these experiences influence your perspective on setbacks or changes in plans?

6. How do you cope with the uncertainty or unpredictability of God's guidance, especially when His plans don't align with yours? Whose plans do you go with most often—yours or God's? What strategies can you adopt to foster trust and acceptance in these situations?

NAVIGATING YOUR JOURNEY:

1. Embrace openness. Being open to God's guidance is the first step in discerning His will for you. Embrace changes, even if they lead you away from your well-laid plans. This might require

stepping out of your comfort zone, but remember, God's plans always lead to a greater purpose.

2. Cultivate attentiveness. Pay attention to the different ways God might be communicating with you. This could be through a dream, a circumstance, an intuition or someone else's advice. Developing an observant and reflective mindset will help you discern His guidance in these diverse forms.

3. Prayer and meditation. Set aside regular time for prayer and meditation. This helps quiet the mind and creates a conducive environment for perceiving His guidance. Share your concerns and seek His direction during these quiet moments.

4. Seek wise counsel. Don't hesitate to seek advice from trusted individuals such as spiritual mentors, pastors or mature believers when trying to discern God's guidance. Their wisdom, experience and objectivity can provide valuable insight.

5. Immediate obedience. Once you've discerned God's guidance, act on it promptly. Remember that delayed obedience can sometimes lead to missed opportunities.

6. Study scriptures. God often speaks to us through His Word. Regular study of the scriptures can provide guidance and direction for your life. Passages like the one from Acts 16:6-10 offer examples of divine guidance and provide a framework to understand God's leading in your life.

7. Trust the journey. God's plans may not always align with ours, and His timeline can often differ from what we have in mind. Trust that His guidance will unfold in the right way and at the right time. Patience and faith go hand-in-hand. They are crucial to navigating your journey under His direction.

THE PATH OF DIVINE guidance is not always a straight line. There will be twists, turns and unexpected detours. But these are all part of the journey that God is leading you on. Trust His navigation, even when the way is unclear.

Day 20: The Harvest of Generosity

FOCUS:

Gratitude

SONG:

Lean on Me – Bill Withers

INTRODUCTION:

IN 2 CORINTHIANS 9:6-15, we are set to explore a topic that reaches beyond the surface: the way generosity fuels gratitude. This isn't just about sharing physical possessions or financial donations; it's about embracing a spirit of giving, which kindles a profound sense of thankfulness in ourselves and others. These verses are not merely instructive, but rather, they challenge us to self-reflect, inspiring us to nurture a lifestyle of generosity. This rich generosity, as depicted in the scripture, ultimately paves the way for a deeper sense of gratitude.

READING:

2 Corinthians 9:6-15 (NLT)

REMEMBER THIS—A FARMER who plants only a few seeds will get a small crop. But the one who plants generously will get a generous crop. You must each decide in your heart how much to give. And don't give reluctantly or in response to pressure. For God loves a person who gives cheerfully. And God will generously provide all you need. Then you will always have everything you need and plenty left over to share with others. As the Scriptures say, "They share freely and give generously to the poor. Their good deeds will be remembered forever."

For God is the one who provides seed for the farmer and then bread to eat. In the same way, he will provide and increase your resources and then produce a great harvest of generosity in you. Yes, you will be enriched in every way so that you can always be generous. And when we take your gifts to those who need them, they

103

will thank God. So two good things will result from this ministry of giving—the needs of the believers in Jerusalem will be met, and they will joyfully express their thanks to God.

As a result of your ministry, they will give the glory to God. For your generosity to them and to all believers will prove that you are obedient to the Good News Of Christ. And they will pray for you with deep affection because of the overflowing grace God has given to you. Thank God for this gift too wonderful for words.

KEY PRINCIPLES:

1. **Cheerful Giving is Encouraged:** Giving should not be a reluctant obligation or done under pressure. God appreciates a cheerful giver, indicating that the spirit of joy in giving is more valuable than the amount given.

2. **Generosity Amplifies Abundance:** Just as a farmer who sows bountifully reaps a plentiful harvest, so does a generous giver find abundance in their life. This principle isn't limited to material wealth; God ensures that the giver's generosity is reciprocated with an increase in spiritual and emotional blessings. This cycle cultivates a 'harvest of generosity' within the giver and their community.

3. **Generosity Meets Needs:** Generous giving helps meet the needs of others, especially those within the community of faith. This practical aspect of generosity demonstrates love in action, as it provides for the necessities of others and directly impacts their lives.

4. **Generosity Evokes Gratitude and Praise:** Generosity doesn't just meet material needs—it sparks gratitude toward God in the receiver's heart. This leads to joyful thanks and glory being given to God, reflecting the positive spiritual impact of generous actions.

5. **Generosity Demonstrates Obedience to the Gospel:** Generosity toward others is a tangible demonstration of a person's obedience to the teachings of Christ. It embodies the message of the Gospel in practical terms, showing God's love in action.

6. **Gratitude Goes Beyond Words:** The gratitude inspired by generosity transcends verbal expression—it creates a spiritual bond, evokes prayers of blessing and strengthens the community of believers.

7. **Generosity is a Divine Gift:** The ability and willingness to be generous are gifts from God. Recognizing and appreciating this can foster a deeper sense of gratitude in ourselves and others.

CONCLUSION:

In the heart of 2 Corinthians 9:6-15 lies a powerful lesson on the cyclical relationship between generosity and gratitude. The scripture presents a vivid metaphor of agricultural sowing and reaping, symbolizing that cheerful and generous giving leads to a rich harvest of blessings. It emphasizes that generosity is more than a physical act; it's an embodiment of a loving and grateful spirit, a lifestyle that invites abundance.

The passage underscores the significance of the intention behind our giving - a cheerful giver finds favor with God. This kind of joyful generosity extends its impact beyond the act itself, nurturing gratitude, strengthening community bonds and enriching the giver and receiver in many ways.

Finally, the scripture reveals God as the ultimate Giver, the source of our resources and the instigator of our generosity. This understanding deepens our gratitude and fuels our willingness to share. By cultivating this cycle of generosity and gratitude, we can realize a bountiful harvest in our lives and communities, bearing testament to the divine wisdom woven into these holy words.

REFLECTION:

1. How have you experienced God's provision after demonstrating generosity? Can you share a story of when you've seen a "harvest of generosity" in your life?
2. Have you ever observed your acts of generosity leading others to express gratitude to God? Can you share these experiences and how they affected your perspective on giving?
3. How do you decide how much to give, whether it's money, time or effort? How do you think this aligns with the teachings of the scripture?
4. Looking at your daily life, how could you integrate a spirit of generosity in non-monetary ways such as time, skills or encouragement?
5. Are there any obstacles that make it challenging for you to be generous? How could you approach these barriers?
6. Reflecting on the scripture's final line: "Thank God for this gift too wonderful for words." This statement expresses deep gratitude for the miraculous power of generosity. How have your experiences with giving and receiving generosity stirred a similar sense of profound gratitude within you?

_____

PRAYER:

DEAR GOD, THANK YOU for opening my heart and mind to the powerful lesson of generosity and gratitude today. I am deeply moved by the understanding that each act of giving is a seed that brings forth a rich harvest of blessings in my life and the lives of others.

Please help me to give cheerfully and abundantly, free from reluctance or pressure. Teach me to recognize that the resources I possess are gifts from You and are meant to be shared with those in need. Show me that through my generosity, I am following the teachings of Christ and manifesting His love in a tangible way.

When I encounter obstacles to generosity, remind me, Father, that You are the ultimate provider, the source of my abundance. Give me faith in your promise that You will always provide for me and increase my resources so that I may, in turn, be a generous giver.

May my generosity inspire others to give thanks and praise to You, thereby strengthening our community of faith. Help me to appreciate that this cycle of giving and receiving, of gratitude and love, is a divine gift too wonderful for words.

As I strive to cultivate a lifestyle of generosity, I ask for Your guidance and grace. May the joy of giving become a deep-seated part of who I am, stirring profound gratitude within me and those I share with.

Thank You, Lord, for the wisdom found in Your holy words today. May it resonate within me and guide me as I strive to live out the spirit of generosity you so beautifully depict.

In Jesus' name, I pray. Amen.

GOING DEEPER:

1. The Bible frequently uses agricultural metaphors like sowing and reaping because they were relevant and understood in the historical context of the people with whom the illustrations were shared. In our modern times, consider the metaphor of 'investing and yielding' in the context of building relationships or community. Just as one who invests time, effort and care into their relationships or community yields a rich harvest of love, support and companionship, how can this concept relate to the principle of generosity in your life? Can you identify any instances of this dynamic at play in your personal relationships or your community? How does the 'harvest' from these investments enrich your life?

2. The scripture encourages generous giving, but what happens when you are the one in need? How do you respond when you're on the receiving end of generosity? When facing financial difficulties, how do you manage your desire to be generous? Are there non-financial ways you've discovered to express your generosity?

3. Generosity is a virtue that often brings joy and fulfillment. However, it can become challenging in a world where some individuals may constantly take without giving back. How do you maintain a spirit of generosity when dealing with people who seem to be continually taking,

potentially crossing into greed or exploiting your kindness? How do you navigate these situations without losing your joy of giving while protecting your emotional and financial well-being?

4. We live in a society where acts of generosity are often publicly recognized and applauded. Reflect on your motivations when you give. Are you ever tempted to give more for the sake of recognition rather than out of genuine generosity? How do you navigate these feelings, and what steps can you take to ensure your giving remains sincere and not influenced by the desire for accolades?

5. How do you handle situations where your generosity isn't acknowledged or seems unappreciated? Does it affect your willingness to give in the future? Reflect on the scripture's focus on cheerful giving as an end in itself. How does this perspective influence your understanding of these experiences?

6. How do you reconcile the call to be generous with the need to be wise and discerning about where your resources are going? How should we respond when we encounter instances where our generosity might be misused or exploited, such as fraudulent charities or insincere requests?

NAVIGATING YOUR JOURNEY:

1. Start with gratitude. Gratitude fosters generosity. Regularly acknowledge and express thanks for the blessings in your life. This could be as simple as maintaining a gratitude journal where you jot down daily things you're grateful for.

2. Give thoughtfully. Generosity is not just about giving freely but also about giving wisely. Before making a donation or offering help, take the time to research and ensure that your resources are going to a legitimate and impactful cause.

3. Give your time and talents. If financial giving is currently a challenge, remember that generosity extends beyond monetary donations. Volunteering your time, sharing your skills or lending an ear to someone in need are all valuable expressions of generosity.

4. Maintain boundaries. While fostering a generous spirit, maintaining personal boundaries is equally important, especially with those who may continuously take without giving back. Giving should not lead to burnout or financial distress.

5. Give without expectations. It can be disheartening when our generosity goes unnoticed or seems unappreciated. However, true generosity is giving without expecting anything in return. Focus on the joy of giving itself rather than the recognition it may or may not bring.

6. Pray for discernment. Pray regularly for wisdom in your acts of generosity. Ask God to guide your decisions and help you strike a balance between being a cheerful giver and a wise steward of your resources.

As you continue this journey, remember that generosity is a heartfelt response to the grace we have received, and it's a journey of growth. It might not always be easy, but by taking these steps, you'll deepen your understanding of generosity and strengthen your capacity to give. These practices will lead you to a more enriching life and enable you to make a more profound impact on the world around you.

Day 21: Immersed in Christ: Living in the Richness of His Message

---

FOCUS:

Wisdom

SONG:

Speak Life – TobyMac

INTRODUCTION:

ON DAY 21, WE INVITE you to delve into the concept of wisdom. Wisdom is not simply about knowledge; it involves understanding and applying that knowledge in the practical realities of life. Our reading today, Colossians 3:16, focuses on letting the Word of Christ—the truest form of wisdom—dwell within us. As we explore this scripture, let's consider how we can apply this wisdom in our lives and relationships.

READING:

Colossians 3:16 (NLT)

Let the message about Christ, in all its richness, fill your lives. Teach and counsel each other with all the wisdom he gives. Sing psalms and hymns and spiritual songs to God with thankful hearts.

KEY PRINCIPLES:

1. **The Richness of Christ's Message:** The scripture emphasizes that the wisdom found in the teaching of Christ is not only profound but also rich and encompassing. It's meant to fill our lives, providing guidance, comfort and insight.
2. **Community Teaching and Counseling:** The passage underscores the importance of community within the faith. Believers are encouraged to teach and counsel one another, utilizing the wisdom that comes from Christ. This fosters a sense of unity and shared growth in understanding.

3. **Wisdom as a Divine Gift:** Wisdom is presented as a gift from Christ, a divine endowment that enables us to navigate life's complexities. It's not merely human intelligence or skill but a more profound understanding that aligns with God's will and purpose.

4. **Gratitude, Worship and Holistic Engagement with Christ's Wisdom:** This principle invites us to let the message of Christ fill our lives in all its richness and to express this through joyful worship and thanksgiving. It emphasizes not just understanding and applying Christ's wisdom but also celebrating it through songs of praise, hymns and spiritual songs. Engaging with the Word of Christ in this way integrates the mind, soul and spirit, creating a holistic connection with God's wisdom and fostering a deep appreciation for all that He provides.

5. **Application of Wisdom:** The wisdom given by Christ is not just for personal edification but is meant to be applied in our interactions and relationships. It's a practical wisdom that guides how we relate to and support one another in our faith journey.

CONCLUSION:

In Colossians 3:16, we find an invitation not merely to know the wisdom of Christ but to let it dwell within us richly, permeating every aspect of our lives. It's not a static understanding but a dynamic, living relationship with the Word, expressed through teaching, counseling, singing and thanksgiving. This scripture challenges us to see wisdom not as a distant intellectual pursuit but as an intimate and holistic connection with God's truth. It's a call to celebrate the richness of Christ's message with our whole selves, engaging our minds, hearts, and spirits. Through this holistic approach, we can cultivate a profound sense of gratitude and joy that resonates in our daily lives, enriching our interactions with others and deepening our relations with God. In a world where knowledge can be cold and disconnected, this scripture reminds us that true wisdom is warm, relational, and rooted in love, guiding us to live with authenticity, compassion, and grace.

REFLECTION:

1. How do you actively allow the wisdom of Christ to dwell within you? What practices or habits have you adopted to cultivate a deeper understanding of God's Word?
2. Have you ever found yourself in a position where you could teach or counsel others using the wisdom you've gained from your relationship with Christ? How did that experience shape your understanding and appreciation of God's wisdom?
3. How do you express gratitude and worship in your spiritual life? What role do songs, hymns or other artistic expressions play in your connection with God?
4. Do you find that your engagement with scripture involves not just your intellect but also your emotions and spirit? How can you deepen this holistic connection with God's Word?
5. Consider a recent interaction with a friend, family member or colleague where you could have applied the wisdom of Christ but did not. How might that wisdom have changed the outcome or the nature of the relationship?
6. What obstacles or challenges have you faced in trying to live out the wisdom of Christ in your daily life? How can you overcome these challenges to allow His message to fill your life more fully?
7. How do you ensure that your pursuit of knowledge and wisdom doesn't become cold or disconnected but remains rooted in love and compassion? What practices might help you maintain this balance?

PRAYER:

Father, I come before You today with a heart yearning for wisdom, the true wisdom that comes only from You. May Your Word dwell richly within me, guiding my thoughts, actions and decisions. Help me understand Your teachings and apply them in my daily life, showing compassion and love to those around me.

Lord, I am grateful for the wisdom You've imparted to me, and I seek to share it with others. Grant me the grace to teach and counsel those in need with kindness and empathy, reflecting Your love in all that I do.

I also seek to express my gratitude and praise through joyful worship. Whether through songs, prayers or silent reflection, may my worship connect me more deeply with You, integrating my mind, soul and spirit in profound appreciation for Your wisdom and grace.

Father, I know that wisdom is a journey, and I need Your guidance every step of the way. When I face challenges or obstacles, remind me to turn to You, trusting that You will provide the insight and strength I need.

Thank You for the richness of Your Word and the opportunity to grow in wisdom and faith. May my life be a testament to Your love and wisdom, and may I always seek to glorify You with a thankful heart.

In Jesus' name, I pray. Amen.

GOING DEEPER:

1. In this passage, the term "richness" refers to depth, complexity and valuable quality. How does this richness influence your beliefs, behaviors or interactions with others? Can you share examples of how these qualities of depth, complexity and value are evident in your spiritual life, relationships or daily practices?
2. In a world where the term "rich" often relates to material wealth, how does the concept of richness in the passage differ from worldly perceptions of wealth? How can you embody this spiritual richness in your life, moving beyond societal views of success? What actions or attitudes can help you nurture this unique richness in your relationship with God and others?
3. Some people today may feel disconnected from hymns and psalms, seeing them as old-fashioned, while others deeply connect with modern praise, worship and gospel music. How can you appreciate and find spiritual richness in traditional and contemporary worship expressions? What is each form's unique value and wisdom, and how can they complement each other in your spiritual journey? If you've felt disconnected from one style of worship, what steps might you take to explore and connect with praise and worship music in a way that resonates with your spiritual needs and preferred expressions?
4. In a rapidly changing world with evolving moral and ethical landscapes, how do you see the wisdom of Christ fitting into contemporary society? What challenges or opportunities does this present for you as a follower of Christ?
5. Have you ever encountered misunderstandings or misapplications of biblical wisdom in your own life or others? How can you address these misconceptions with grace and truth, aligning with the authentic wisdom of Christ?

NAVIGATING YOUR JOURNEY:

1. Embrace richness beyond wealth. Begin by reflecting on the difference between material wealth and spiritual richness. Spend time meditating on the depth, complexity and valuable

quality of Christ's message and how you can embody this richness in your daily life.

2. Engage with diverse worship forms. Explore both traditional hymns and psalms as well as modern praise and worship music. Create a playlist that mixes both styles and use it during your personal worship time. Consider attending different worship services that emphasize various musical expressions.

3. Apply wisdom in relationships. Intentionally consider how the wisdom of Christ could impact your daily interactions with friends, family and colleagues. Seek opportunities to practice compassion, empathy and grace, guided by Christ's teachings.

4. Cultivate a holistic connection with God's Word. Engage your mind, emotions and spirit as you study scripture. Consider keeping a journal where you can write your thoughts, feelings and questions as you read. This can foster a deeper and more personal understanding of God's Word.

5. Seek community and mentorship. Connect with others in your faith community who can support your growth in wisdom. Consider joining a small group or seeking a mentor to guide and encourage you on your spiritual journey.

6. Explore the timeless wisdom of hymns and psalms. If you find yourself disconnected from hymns and psalms, try exploring their historical context and the profound spiritual insights they contain. These expressions of worship often carry layers of meaning and wisdom that reflect the experiences, hopes and faith of past generations. You might also collaborate with others to create modern renditions or interpretations that resonate with you, connecting with both the rich spiritual heritage they represent and your contemporary spiritual practices.

Navigating the journey toward a deeper wisdom requires a mindful and intentional approach. By exploring the richness of Christ's message, engaging with various forms of worship and embracing wisdom as a lifelong journey, you can cultivate a profound and practical faith. Remember, the wisdom of Christ is not a destination but an ongoing relationship that enriches every aspect of your life.

Day 22: Empowered and Authorized for Kingdom Impact: Spreading the Good News

---

FOCUS:

Guidance

SONG:

Worth Fighting For – Brian Courtney Wilson

INTRODUCTION:

MATTHEW 28:19-20 IS both a call to action and a demonstration of faith. It is an invitation to spread the teachings of Christ to every corner of the earth. While serving as a reminder of our duty, this passage also assures us of a comforting truth: we are never alone in our endeavors. His presence emboldens us to live out these teachings no matter where our journeys take us.

READING:

Matthew 28:19-20 (NLT)

Therefore, go and make disciples of all the nations, baptizing them in the name of the Father and the Son and the Holy Spirit. Teach these new disciples to obey all the commands I have given you. And be sure of this: I am with you always, even to the end of the age.

KEY PRINCIPLES:

1. **The Great Commission:** This passage is often referred to as the Great Commission, where Jesus commands His followers to spread the Gospel and make disciples of all nations. It's a clear directive for believers to actively engage in evangelism and discipleship.
2. **Baptism in the Triune God:** Jesus mentions baptism in the name of the Father, the Son and the Holy Spirit. This highlights the importance of baptism as a sign of initiation into the Christian faith. It also accentuated the central Christian doctrine of the Trinity.
3. **Teaching and Obedience:** There is a focus on not only spreading the word but also teaching

new disciples to obey Jesus' commands. This emphasizes that faith in Christ involves not merely a belief but a commitment to live according to His teachings.

4. **Universal Outreach:** Jesus' commands is to make disciples of all nations, emphasizing that the message of Christianity is universal and meant for all people, regardless of their cultural, ethnic or geographical background.

5. **Assurances of Jesus' Presences:** The closing promise, "I am with you always, even to the end of the age," provides assurance of Jesus' constant presence with His followers. This is a source of encouragement and strength, knowing that in fulfilling this great task, believers are not alone.

6. **Mission in Everyday Life:** The command to "go and make disciples of all nations" isn't limited to professional missionaries or those who travel abroad for evangelism. It's a call to all believers to live out and share their faith wherever they are, recognizing that every place they step is a potential mission field. This principle reinforces that the task of sharing the Gospel and living according to Christ's teachings is a daily commitment and opportunity, not confined to locations or circumstances.

CONCLUSION:

The Great Commission, as outlined in Mathew 28:19-20 isn't just a task assigned to a select few; it's a calling that resonates with every believer, in every place and at all times. It broadens our understanding of mission, turning our everyday environments into fields ripe for sharing Christ's love. The emphasis on baptism, teaching, obedience and universal outreach reflects a multifaced approach to faith that goes beyond mere proclamation to include nurturing, inclusion and commitment to living out Christ's teachings Perhaps most reassuringly, this passage extends an unbreakable promise of Jesus' presence, offering a sense of companionship and strength as we navigate the complexities of life and faith.

It invites us to see our world through a missionary lens, challenging us to be active participants in a global community of faith, all the while knowing that we do not walk alone. This message is a powerful reminder that our faith is not a private or isolated journey but a dynamic, communal and universal call to action, guided and supported by the unwavering presence of Christ Himself.

REFLECTION:

1. How do you personally interpret the command to "go and make disciples"? Consider that you don't have to be a minister or evangelist to fulfill this calling. You may be someone who plants seeds of faith, even if you don't always see the harvest. What steps can you take to plant and water those seeds in your daily life, recognizing that someone else may see the fruits of your labor – and that is perfectly okay?

2. Reflect on your understanding of baptism and the Trinity. How do these concepts connect with your personal faith journey? What significance do they hold for you?

3. Reflect on the balance between sharing faith and teaching obedience to Christ's commands. Too much focus on sharing faith without teaching obedience may lead to a shallow understanding of what it means to be a disciple of Christ. How can you personally ensure that your approach to evangelism includes not only grace but also a call to transformation and holiness?

4. Conversely, consider the risk of overemphasizing obedience without sharing the love and grace of Christ. This can become legalistic and may turn away people struggling with faith or other specific issues. How can you actively engage in teaching obedience to Christ's commands while also demonstrating compassion, understanding and grace?

5. How can you make an effort to understand and connect with people from different cultures, backgrounds or beliefs in the context of sharing the Gospel? What barriers might you need to overcome?

6. Think about moments when you have felt alone or overwhelmed in your faith journey. How might the promise of Jesus' constant presence inspire or comfort you in those times?

7. Think about your daily routine and surroundings. Where do you see opportunities to share your faith or live according to Christ's teachings? How can you cultivate a mindset that views every interaction as a potential mission field?

8. How does the message of this scripture resonate with your personal experiences and current stage in your spiritual journey? Are there areas where you feel challenged or encouraged to grow?

PRAYER:

Gracious Heavenly Father, I come before you with a heart filled with gratitude and a desire to answer Your call. The Great Commission is not just a distant command but a personal invitation, one that You've extended to me right here and now.

Lord, I confess that sometimes I feel inadequate or overwhelmed by the task of sharing Your love and teachings. But I'm reminded that I don't have to be an expert, a minister or an evangelist. You've called me to plant seeds, to be a witness to Your grace and to reflect Your love in every interaction.

Please help me to find the right balance between sharing faith and teaching obedience, between offering grace and calling for transformation. Guide me to approach others with compassion and understanding, to see beyond barriers and to connect with people from all walks of life.

Strengthen me to see my everyday surroundings as opportunities, as fields ripe for Your love. Open my eyes to see those chances to share my faith and open my heart to love as You love, to serve as You serve.

Most of all, Lord, let me be mindful of Your promise to be with me always. Your presence is my comfort, my strength and my guide. Even when I feel alone or overwhelmed, I know that You walk beside me, guiding me every step of the way.

May I live out Your Great Commission with joy and passion, with humility and trust, knowing that I am part of Your grand and beautiful purpose, not by my might but by Your Spirit.

In Jesus' name, I pray. Amen.

GOING DEEPER:

1. If "making disciples" is a universal calling for all Christians, how does this align with your unique gifts, talents and circumstances? How might you align our everyday life with this call, even in seemingly small and mundane ways?
2. Reflecting on your spiritual journey thus far, where do you feel the most growth has occurred? Where do you sense a need for further development and challenge? How might you intentionally pursue spiritual maturity in these areas?
3. How does the assurance of Jesus' presence influence your actions, decisions and relationships? How can this assurance shape the way you approach challenges and opportunities?
4. How can the Church as a community avoid the pitfalls of legalism and shallow faith? What role can you personally play in fostering a culture that balances grace with the call to holiness?

5. How can you nurture a deeper, more mature understanding of discipleship in those around you? What might it look like to move beyond mere belief or rule-following to a rich, transformative faith journey?

6. The Bible presents the Holy Spirit as a divine person with a mind, emotions and will, possessing characteristics of God such as omnipresence and omniscience. See Acts 5:3-4; Psalm 139:7-8; 1 Corinthians 2:10-11. https://www.gotquestions.org/who-Holy-Spirit.html

How does this understanding of the Holy Spirit as a personal being rather than a mystical force or impersonal power shape your relationship with God? In what ways do you experience the Holy Spirit's role as Comforter and Counselor in your daily life? Reflect on moments when you have felt the guidance or conviction of the Holy Spirit and consider how this awareness might deepen your faith and dependence on God's presence.

1. The Holy Spirit is described as having diverse roles and functions, from convicting the world regarding sin, righteousness and judgment to taking up permanent residence in the hearts of believers as Helper, Comforter and Guide (John 16:8; John 14:16, Romans 8:9; 1 Corinthians 12:3). Moreover, the Spirit is a revealer of truth, a gift-giver and a fruit-producer in the lives of Christians (John 16:13; 1 Corinthians 12; Galatians 5:22-23). https://www.gotquestions.org/Spirit-today.html

    a. How have you experienced the Holy Spirit's work in convicting you or others about sin and leading you toward salvation? Reflect on how this conviction has shaped our understanding of sin and righteousness.

    b. Consider how the Holy Spirit, living within you, serves as a continual source of encouragement and guidance in your life. How has the Spirit been a Helper or Counselor to you in specific situations?

    c. Explore how the Holy Spirit has guided you into understanding God's Word and His truths. In what ways has the Spirit helped you discern spiritual matters and grow in your relationship with Jesus Christ?

    d. Reflect on the spiritual gifts and fruits of the Spirit that you have recognized in your life or the lives of others. How have these gifts and fruits enabled you to glorify God and serve others?

    e. Meditate on the assurance that the Holy Spirit will never leave or forsake you and that His presence is a cause for joy and comfort. How does this knowledge impact your daily walk with God?

NAVIGATING YOUR JOURNEY:

1. Embrace your role. Understand that "making disciples" isn't reserved for religious leaders alone. Embrace your unique gifts and opportunities to spread Christ's teachings in everyday interactions.

2. Strive for balance. Practice a balanced approach between teaching obedience and sharing faith. Focus on transformation through grace rather than leaning toward legalism or superficial belief.

3. Connect across boundaries. Seek ways to connect with people from various cultural, ethnic or geographical backgrounds. Recognize that the Gospel is universal and strive to bridge any barriers that might hinder your message.

4. Cultivate awareness. Be mindful of your surroundings and view every interaction as a potential mission field. There are opportunities to witness everywhere, from casual conversations to more deliberate engagements.

5. Build a relationship with the Holy Spirit. Develop a personal relationship with the Holy Spirit as a constant guide and comforter. Reflect on how the Spirit is working in your life and how you might be more responsive to His guidance.

6. See spiritual growth. Identify areas where you feel a need for growth in your faith. Consider joining a study group, seeking mentorship or investing in personal study and prayer to deepen your understanding.

7. Share the journey with others. Cultivate a supportive community that encourages each other to live out the Great Commission. Whether through a church group or personal friendships, encouragement and accountability can be vital.

8. Celebrate the assurance of Jesus' presence. Remember that you are never alone on this journey. Lean into the promise of Jesus' constant presence, especially when you feel overwhelmed or uncertain.

The journey to fulfill the Great Commission is both a personal calling and a shared endeavor. It's about aligning our daily lives with Christ's teachings and connecting with others in meaningful and transformative ways. By embracing our unique roles, striving for balance, building relationships and drawing strength from the Holy Spirit, we're not merely navigating this journey; we're actively participating in God's grand purpose, assured of His guidance and presence at every step.

Day 23: Transformed by Christ – Shaping Worries Through Prayer and Praise

FOCUS:

Gratitude

SONG:

Good, Good Father – Chris Tomlin

INTRODUCTION:

Philippians 4:6-9 offers a calming antidote to worry and anxiety, guiding us toward prayer and the peace it brings. It emphasizes the transformative power of reorienting our concerns toward God and embracing a perspective that focuses on the positives in life. As we study these verses, we uncover how cultivating an attitude of gratitude can be a potent remedy to life's worries and troubles.

READING:

Philippians 4:6-9 (MSG)

Don't fret or worry. Instead of worrying, pray. Let petitions and praises shape your worries into prayers, letting God know your concerns. Before you know it, a sense of God's wholeness, everything coming together for good, will come and settle you down. It's wonderful what happens when Christ displaces worry from the center of your life. Summing it all up, friends, I'd say you'll do best by filling your minds and meditating on things true, noble, reputable, authentic, compelling, gracious – the best, not the worst; the beautiful, not the ugly; things to praise, not things to curse. Put into practice what you learned from me, what you heard and saw and realized. Do that, and God, who makes everything work together, will work you into his most excellent harmonies.

KEY PRINCIPLES:

1. **Turning Worry into Prayer:** Instead of succumbing to worry, we are guided to turn our concerns into prayers. It's a shift from focusing on the problem to seeking the one who holds the solution.

2. **Praise as a Weapon Against Anxiety:** Alongside petitions, praise is highlighted as a way

to combat anxiety. When we focus on God's goodness and praise Him amid worries, our perspective changes, and peace becomes accessible.

3. **Promise of God's Peace:** By praying and praising, a sense of God's wholeness and peace will come to settle us down. This peace is not a mere emotion but a divine reality transcending our circumstances.

4. **Focusing on What's Right:** Paul emphasizes meditating on things that are true, noble, reputable, authentic, compelling and gracious. This conscious choice to dwell on the positives rather than the negatives can transform our mindset and elevate our spiritual state.

5. **Practical Application:** This is not just theoretical or abstract teaching. We are called to put these principles – and other instructions elsewhere that we have learned from Paul – into practice. We are to make them a natural part of our daily lives, trusting in God's wisdom and grace.

6. **Christ's Transformative Power:** The scripture emphasizes a holistic approach to life, suggesting that prayer and positive focus can influence our spiritual lives and our mental, emotional and physical well-being. When we allow Christ to displace worry as the center of our lives - by turning worries into prayers and focusing on the good - we align ourselves with a divine plan that brings everything together for our overall benefit.

CONCLUSION:

The teachings from Philippians 4:6-9 do not merely offer a spiritual escapism. Instead, they present a multi-dimensional approach that integrates the spiritual with the mental, emotional and even physical aspects of our being.

It's not just about having blind, passive faith; it's about active engagement with God, where we turn our concerns over to Him and trust in His goodness. By meditating on what is true, noble and beautiful, we can cultivate a mindset that guards against anxiety and discontent.

The passage also emphasizes the importance of putting what we learn into practice, creating a harmonious rhythm in our lives that aligns with God's will. It's a practical and spiritual guide that can lead us to a more content and peaceful state, not just spiritually but mentally and emotionally as well.

In the hustle and bustle of our modern times, these verses serve as a gentle reminder that there's a higher way to live—one that doesn't merely cope with life's difficulties but transcends them. It's a path that takes us beyond mere survival to a place of thriving, guided by divine wisdom and grounded in an unshakeable peace.

REFLECTION:

1. How do you typically react when you feel anxious or worried? Have you ever tried turning your worries into prayers? What might that process look like for you?
2. Can you recall a time when you praised God even during a difficult or worrisome situation? How did it change your perspective or emotional state?
3. How do you currently experience God's peace in your life? Are there specific practices or thoughts that help you connect with His peace?
4. Consider your thought patterns and where your mind usually wanders. How can you intentionally shift your focus to meditate on true, noble, reputable, authentic, compelling and gracious things?
5. Reflect on the ways you currently cope with life's difficulties. How can you move from merely surviving to thriving, following the guidance in this passage? What does thriving look like for you?
6. How can you integrate the spiritual teachings from this passage with the mental, emotional and physical aspects of your being? Can you identify areas where these aspects are in harmony within you? Or places where they may need realignment?
7. How can you ensure that your faith is not passive but an active engagement with God? What practices or disciplines could help you cultivate a more dynamic faith?

PRAYER:

Heavenly Father, in the stillness of this moment, I come before You, weighed down by the worries and anxieties that so often cloud my mind. But, here, in Your presence, I find solace and strength and am reminded of Your everlasting love and faithfulness.

Lord, teach me to turn my worries into prayers, to lay down my burdens at Your feet, trusting that You hold the solutions to every problem. Help me to praise You, even during uncertainty, for You are good and Your graciousness knows no bounds.

May Your peace, which surpasses all understanding, settle my heart and calm my soul. Guide me to meditate on what is true, noble and beautiful, shifting my focus from the chaos of life to the serenity found in You.

Empower me to put into practice the teachings of Your word, to not just survive but to thrive. Align my thoughts, emotions and actions with Your divine plan so that I may be a vessel of Your love and peace in this world.

I thank You, Father, for Your unwavering guidance and the promise that everything comes together for good when Christ is at the center of my life. May I walk in Your wisdom, grounded in an unshakeable peace, knowing that You are with me every step of the way.

In Jesus' name, I pray. Amen.

GOING DEEPER:

1. In the face of real devastation, the command to "be anxious for nothing" can seem almost unattainable. How can you reconcile this scriptural guidance with the very real emotions of fear, worry and grief that devastating experiences bring? What does it mean for you personally to trust God amid profound pain without expecting instant resolution or easy answers?

2. What role can the community of believers play in supporting and encouraging one another? How can you cultivate relationships that allow for authentic sharing of struggles and mutual support in faith?

3. Think about ways you may unconsciously rehearse or memorize your pain, troubles or anguish. How has this practice shaped your perspective, emotions and daily life? What barriers or fears might be preventing you from releasing these rehearsed narratives and focusing on the noble, true and beautiful? Is there ever a point where holding on to them consumes or harms you (or those around you) more than it helps you?

4. Recognizing that emotions are complex and multifaceted; how can you balance the need to acknowledge and process genuine pain and suffering with the call to meditate on positive and uplifting truths? How can you tell when you are authentically dealing with pain versus when you might be trapped in a cycle of rehearsing it? What spiritual practices, community support or personal insights might help you navigate this delicate balance?

5. Have you ever found yourself using "waiting on the Lord" as a cover for fear, complacency or indecision? How do you differentiate between genuinely seeking God's guidance and simply avoiding action? What obstacles have you had to overcome to move from passive waiting to active engagement with God? What was the result of making that shift?

6. How do you reconcile the idea of trusting God's plan with the responsibility to act on your faith? Have you ever felt God urging you to make a move but resisted out of fear or comfort with your current situation? How did you eventually respond, and what impact did that decision have on your faith journey? What steps can you take to ensure that your faith is not merely a comforting concept but a compelling call to action?

7. In pursuing an active faith, how do you ensure that you are not simply imposing your will or desires but truly aligning with God's purposes? How do you navigate the fine line between taking initiative and relinquishing control? Are there experiences where you've either rushed

ahead or lagged behind God's timing? What painful or transformative lessons have those experiences taught you?

8. How does the community of believers around you support or challenge your move from passive to active faith? Have there been times when communal pressures either stifled your initiatives or pushed you too aggressively? How did you find the right balance? What role do honesty, accountability and discernment play in your communal faith journey?

NAVIGATING YOUR JOURNEY:

1. Evaluate your environment. Identify if you are part of any relationships, whether friends, significant others, family, colleagues or even church communities, which may be contributing to unhealthy patterns or spiritual stagnation. If you find yourself in any unhealthy relationship, pray for guidance and have the courage to leave if it is detrimental to your well-being. Remember, not all who say "Lord" genuinely know Him. Seek out a church or community that nurtures your faith and encourages healthy growth. Look for signs of authenticity, compassion and alignment with Christ's teachings.

2. Recognize and address rehearsing pain. Note when and how you repeatedly recall painful memories or troubles and how it affects your daily life. If rehearsing pain becomes overwhelming, consider counseling or therapy rooted in spiritual wisdom. Focus on the present moment and cultivate gratitude for the blessings in your life. With prayer and positive focus, work to release old, painful narratives and embrace new, healing perspectives that align with God's love and truth. Lean on friends, family and spiritual leaders who can provide encouragement and perspective when you find yourself stuck in rehearsing pain.

3. If you're struggling with suicidal thoughts, seek professional help immediately. You can call, text or chat 988 for the Suicide & Crisis lifeline. In the U.S., the National Suicide Prevention Lifeline can be reached at 1-800-273-TALK (1-800-273-8255). You can also call, text or chat 988 for the Suicide & Crisis lifeline. Or use the Crisis Text Line by texting HOME to 741741. You are not alone; there are people ready and willing to help.

4. Understand that anxiety, worry, and stress are real experiences that can sometimes be overwhelming. God doesn't discourage us from seeking help; in fact, He provides assistance. If your worries or anxieties feel too heavy to bear alone, don't hesitate to contact a trusted friend, counselor, therapist, or other professional. God works through people and these resources to provide comfort and guidance.

5. Identify moments of passive faith. Reflect on times when you might have been "waiting on the Lord" as a cover for complacency or indecision. Acknowledge these moments and ask for wisdom and courage to move from passive waiting to active engagement.

6. Cultivate an active prayer life. Instead of worrying, practice turning concerns into prayers and praises. Regularly spend time in God's presence, allowing His peace to calm your anxieties. Prayer journals or prayer partners can help facilitate this practice.

7. Embrace praise in difficult times. Actively chose to praise God even during hardships. Engaging in worship, reading uplifting scriptures or maintaining a gratitude journal can foster a mindset of praise.

8. Build a supportive community. Surround yourself with friends and believers who encourage active faith. Accountability, honesty and shared goals can create an environment that motivates positive spiritual growth.

9. Align your actions with divine purposes. Regularly seek God's guidance through prayer, scripture reading and seeking wise counsel to ensure that your initiatives align with His will rather than your desires.

10. Integrate spiritual teaching with all aspects of life. Pursue a balanced approach that integrates spiritual principles with mental, emotional and physical well-being. Engage in practices like prayer, meditation, fasting, study, service or worship alongside therapy or wellness practices to align your whole being with spiritual truth.

11. Commit to thriving, not just surviving. Create a personal vision for what thriving means to you, rooted in scripture and holy wisdom. Utilize tools like a vision board, journaling goals, engaging in regular self-reflection, joining a supportive group – perhaps a small group, or seeking mentorship. Setting specific goals, monitoring progress and celebrating victories will support this journey from mere survival to flourishing.

Embarking on this spiritual journey requires intention, courage and commitment to growth. By actively engaging these principles and embracing both divine guidance and community support, you are taking purposeful strides toward a fulfilled, well-balanced life in Christ. Continue to seek God's wisdom, nourish your faith and remain open to transformation, for this path is not a destination but an ongoing journey toward deeper understanding, love and fulfillment.

Day 24: Discovering the Source of Wisdom: Embracing the Fear of the Lord

FOCUS:

Wisdom

SONG:

First Things First – Consumed By Fire

INTRODUCTION:

JOB 28:20-28 PAINTS a vivid picture of the pursuit of wisdom and insight. This passage reminds us that these virtues, much like the gratitude that blooms from generosity, aren't merely attained through human effort. They're gifts from God, whose infinite understanding surpasses our own. These verses urge us to respect and recognize the divine, emphasizing that true wisdom and understanding come from a healthy reverence of the Lord and a conscious decision to shun evil.

READING:

Job 28:20-28 (MSG)

So where does Wisdom come from? And where does Insight live? It can't be found by looking, no matter how deep you dig, no matter how high you fly. If you search through the graveyard and question the dead, they say, 'We've only heard rumors of it.'

God alone knows the way to Wisdom, he knows the exact place to find it. He knows where everything is on earth, he sees everything under heaven. After he commanded the winds to blow and measured out the waters, Arranged for the rain and set off explosions of thunder and lightning, He focused on Wisdom, made sure it was all set and tested and ready. Then he addressed the human race: 'Here it is! Fear-of-the-Lord—that's Wisdom, and Insight means shunning evil.'

KEY PRINCIPLES:

1. **The Elusiveness of Wisdom and Insight:** The text begins by illustrating how wisdom and

insight are beyond human reach. No matter how deep one digs or high one flies, these virtues cannot be attained through human effort alone. They are not to be found in the material world or through our own intelligence.

2. **Wisdom as a Divine Gift:** The passage makes it clear that wisdom is a gift from God. Only God knows where wisdom resides and has the ability to reveal it. Human beings can't obtain it through their own devices.

3. **God's Sovereignty and Omnipotence:** This scripture emphasizes God's control over the natural world. His command of the winds, waters, rain, thunder and lightning illustrates his supreme power and authority over creation.

4. **Wisdom as a Creation by God:** God didn't just discover wisdom; He created and tested it. It is part of His divine plan, carefully constructed and given to humanity.

5. **The Fear of the Lord as the Beginning of Wisdom:** The passage culminates in the revelation that the beginning of wisdom is the fear of the Lord. This is not a terror or dread but a profound respect and awe for the divine. Recognizing God's supremacy and living in reverence toward Him is depicted as the pathway to true wisdom.

6. **Insight as Shunning Evil:** The passage also emphasizes that insight is tied to a moral choice – shunning evil. It implies that true understanding and wisdom involve living a righteous life.

7. **Humanity's Dependence on Divine Revelation:** The scripture underscores that humanity depends on God to reveal wisdom. Without God's revelation, we are like the dead who have only heard rumors of wisdom.

CONCLUSION:

The passage from Job 28:20-28 goes beyond a simple lesson about the pursuit of wisdom and insight. It invites us to reflect on the elusiveness of these virtues, not to deter us but to guide us toward a higher understanding. The scripture subtly warns us against relying solely on our intellect or earthly endeavors to attain wisdom. Instead, it directs us to recognize the divine source of true wisdom.

In an age where information is abundant, yet wisdom often seems scarce, this passage challenges us to shift our focus from mere human effort to a profound reverence for the Lord. It encourages us to see beyond the surface and to align our pursuits with spiritual principles. By shunning evil and cultivating a healthy fear of the Lord, we embark on a path that may lead us to the very wisdom and insight that seem so elusive.

The timeless teachings found in these verses are not merely historical or philosophical ideas but living principles that can guide our daily lives. They remind us that the pursuit of wisdom is not just a personal quest but a spiritual journey that requires humility, reverence and an understanding of our place in the grand scheme of things. This script doesn't just offer answers; it provokes questions, pushing us to examine what true wisdom means in our lives and how we might strive to attain it in harmony with our Creator.

REFLECTION:

1. In today's world, knowledge is often equated with wisdom, but the passage reveals that true wisdom begins with a profound respect and awe for the divine. How do you define wisdom in your daily life, and how does that definition align or contrast with the divine wisdom described in this passage?

2. Reflect on the "fear of the Lord" concept as the beginning of wisdom. How do you interpret this "fear," and how does it manifest in your relationship with God? How might this reverential fear guide your choices and behavior?

3. In our personal quests for wisdom, we often rely on our own skills, knowledge or intuition. Reflect on a time when you attempted to gain insight through these means alone. How did that approach compare to when you sought God first, asking Him to reveal answers to you?

4. Reflecting on the scripture's depiction of God's supreme control over nature, how do you feel about relinquishing control in your own life and trusting in God's supreme ways? Is it difficult for you to let go and trust that His authority is ultimate? How might understanding God's sovereignty over all creation help you surrender control in areas of your life where you struggle? What obstacles, habits, or mindsets get in the way of "letting go and letting God"?

5. The passage associates insight with the moral choice of shunning evil and living righteously. How does this perspective resonate with your understanding of wisdom and morality? Have you ever faced a situation where you had to choose between what was easy and what was right? How did your values and beliefs guide you, and what insights did you gain from that experience? How do you strive to live a life that reflects a commitment to righteousness, and what challenges have you encountered in seeking to shun evil?

6. The lesson describes wisdom as created by God and tested and set by Him. In your pursuit of wisdom, have you ever found yourself testing the wisdom you gained? How do you recognize and discern true wisdom in your life, and what role does faith in God's divine plan play in the process? Reflect on instances where you have sought to understand, apply and even test wisdom, and how understanding wisdom as a divine creation might influence your approach.

7. Some individuals misunderstand the concept of 'fearing the Lord,' associating it with terror or dread, and in some cases, it has even been used abusively to control people. What was your understanding of "the fear of the Lord" before reading this lesson? How does knowing that it means to have a profound respect and awe for Him make you feel?

8. In what ways can you cultivate a healthy, deep reverence toward Him? How can this healthy reverence shape your understanding and pursuit of wisdom? How can recognizing God's supremacy lead you to a path of true wisdom? What steps can you take to deepen this essential aspect of our spiritual journey?

PRAYER:

Gracious and Almighty Father, I stand in awe of Your wisdom and power, so beautifully depicted in the scripture today. My mind is humbled by the realization that Your understanding is far beyond my reach, yet You invite me to partake in Your divine wisdom.

Teach me to seek Your wisdom, not just in knowledge but in reverence and respect for You. Help me to recognize that true insight begins with a healthy fear of You, not terror or dread, but a profound love and awe that guides my every thought and action.

I confess that I have sometimes sought wisdom in my own ways, leaning on my own understanding, and forgetting to turn to You, the Creator and Tester of all wisdom. Forgive me for those times when I have faltered and lead me back to the path that honors You. Help me to shun evil and make moral choices that reflect Your righteousness. As I embark on this spiritual journey, let me not be swayed by worldly temptations but remain focused on You, the source of all wisdom and truth.

Lord, I relinquish control of my life, trusting in Your supreme ways. Even when it is difficult to let go, remind me of Your sovereignty over all creation and guide me to surrender areas where I struggle.

I pray for the strength to live a life that mirrors Your wisdom, to test it, and to apply it in all I do. Fill me with Your insight, grace and understanding so that my pursuit of wisdom may not be a vain chase after the wind but a meaningful journey in harmony with You, my creator.

Thank You, Father, for this profound lesson, for challenging me, for provoking questions in my heart and for guiding me toward a deeper relationship with You.

I pray all this in Jesus' name. Amen

GOING DEEPER:

1. Knowledge is often seen as having facts and information, while Godly wisdom is the understanding and ability to apply knowledge in a righteous and divine way. Reflect on experiences where you've seen both knowledge and wisdom at play. How can knowledge be a helpful tool in your life? Why is Godly wisdom even more essential? In what practical ways

can you seek to grow in knowledge and wisdom, recognizing the stronger connection to God's purpose and plan?

2. Think about a time when the wisdom you gained was tested through trials or adversity. How did these experiences refine your understanding of true wisdom? How did they strengthen or challenge your faith in God's plan?

3. Have you, or someone you know, ever encountered a situation where the concept of "fearing the Lord" or other religious teachings were misused to manipulate or control? Reflect on how these teachings were twisted and how that affected your or the other person's relationship with God or a spiritual community. What insights can be drawn from these personal experiences to foster a genuine and healthy reverence for the divine, free from manipulation or coercion? How can you ensure that your understanding of "fearing the Lord" aligns with a loving and respectful relationship with God?

4. The scripture describes insight as synonymous with shunning evil, while the dictionary definition emphasizes a deep, intuitive understanding of the true nature of things. Reflect on how these two meanings can coexist in your daily life. How can shunning evil become a path to deeper understanding and discernment? How does your faith guide you in recognizing underlying truths? How can you foster a spiritual insight that encompasses both moral righteousness and profound comprehension of the world and yourself?

5. In a society that values self-reliance and personal control, the concept of surrendering to a higher power might feel counterintuitive or even daunting. Reflect on your own experiences with letting go of control and putting your trust in God's wisdom. What challenges have you faced in embracing this surrender? How has this trust enriched your life or brought you peace? What steps can you take to cultivate this trust further and surrender in areas where you may still be holding on?

6. Reflect on experiences in your life where you felt you had to be self-reliant because others let you down or the trust was broken. How have these experiences shaped your relationships and trust in others and a higher power? What steps can you take to rebuild trust and learn to rely on others, including God, without losing a sense of personal responsibility and strength?

7. Reflect on specific times in your life when you sought wisdom, guidance or answers from sources other than God – such as relying solely on human understanding, seeking advice from those who don't have spiritual discernment, or following cultural norms that conflict with holy wisdom. What were the outcomes of those choices? How did those experiences differ from when you sought wisdom through prayer or spiritual guidance? What insights did you gain about the nature of true wisdom and the importance of aligning your pursuit of understanding with God?

NAVIGATING YOUR JOURNEY:

1. Cultivate reverence. Begin with a daily practice of prayer, meditation or quiet reflection to develop a profound respect and awe for God. Allow this time to deepen your understanding of His wisdom.

2. Seek divine guidance first. Before turning to human wisdom or cultural norms, seek God's wisdom through prayer, studying the Scriptures and consulting spiritual mentors who share your faith.

3. Embrace righteous living. Make a conscious effort to shun evil and live righteously. This might mean making difficult choices but knowing that you're aligning yourself with God's principles will strengthen your spiritual path.

4. Relinquish control. Practice letting go of the need to control every aspect of your life. Trust in God's wisdom and sovereignty. Surrendering control can be liberating and lead to a deeper sense of peace.

5. Build trust after brokenness. If you have been let down by others and struggle with trust, consider seeking counseling or spiritual mentorship to heal and rebuild trust. Use discernment when deciding who to share with in the future. Focus on God's unchanging nature as a source of trustworthiness.

6. Use knowledge wisely. Learn to differentiate between worldly knowledge and divine wisdom. Utilize knowledge, but always in alignment with spiritual principles and moral choices.

7. Test and apply wisdom. Don't just accept wisdom passively. Apply it, test it and reflect on its validity in your life. Always align it with God's teachings and principles.

8. Create a supportive community. Surround yourself with friends, family or a faith community who share your pursuit of divine wisdom. This support can enrich your spiritual journey and help you stay on path.

Beginning a journey to discover divine wisdom requires more than intellectual pursuit; it calls for a humble heart, a respectful fear of the Lord and a willingness to align our lives with His principles. By cultivating a daily practice of reverence, seeking God's guidance first, embracing righteous living and building a supportive community, we can navigate our way toward the true wisdom that rises above human understanding. It's a lifelong journey that offers great insight and connection with our Creator, guiding us to live in harmony with His divine plan.

Day 25: From Law to Life: Experiencing Freedom and Transformation Through Christ

FOCUS:

Guidance

SONG:

Speak to My Heart – Donnie McClurkin

INTRODUCTION:

ROMANS 8:3-17 IS A passage rich with reminders of God's extraordinary intervention through Jesus Christ. It delves into the compelling influence of God's Spirit within us, dismantling the bonds of self-obsession and charting a path to a liberated, expansive life.

READING:

Romans 8:3-17 (MSG)

God went for the jugular when He sent His own Son. He didn't deal with the problem as something remote and unimportant. In His Son, Jesus, He personally took on the human condition, entered the disordered mess of struggling humanity in order to set it right once and for all. The law code, weakened as it always was by fractured human nature, could never have done that.

The law always ended up being used as a Band-Aid on sin instead of a deep healing of it. And now what the law code asked for but we couldn't deliver is accomplished as we, instead of redoubling our own efforts, simply embrace what the Spirit is doing in us.

Those who think they can do it on their own end up obsessed with measuring their own moral muscle but never get around to exercising it in real life. Those who trust God's action in them find that God's Spirit is in them—living and breathing God! Obsession with self in these matters is a dead end; attention to God leads us out into the open, into a spacious, free life. Focusing on the self is the opposite of focusing on God. Anyone completely absorbed in self ignores God, ends up thinking more about self than God. That person ignores who God is and what He is doing. And God isn't pleased at being ignored.

But if God himself has taken up residence in your life, you can hardly be thinking more of yourself than of Him. Anyone, of course, who has not welcomed this invisible but clearly present God, the Spirit of Christ, won't know what we're talking about. But for you who welcome Him, in whom He dwells—even though you still experience all the limitations of sin—you yourself experience life on God's terms. It stands to reason, doesn't it, that if the alive-and-present God who raised Jesus from the dead moves into your life, he'll do the same thing in you that he did in Jesus, bringing you alive to himself? When God lives and breathes in you (and he does, as surely as he did in Jesus), you are delivered from that dead life. With his Spirit living in you, your body will be as alive as Christ's!

So don't you see that we don't owe this old do-it-yourself life one red cent. There's nothing in it for us, nothing at all. The best thing to do is give it a decent burial and get on with your new life. God's Spirit beckons. There are things to do and places to go!

This resurrection life you received from God is not a timid, grave-tending life. It's adventurously expectant, greeting God with childlike "What's next, Papa?" God's Spirit touches our spirits and confirms who we really are. We know who he is, and we know who we are: Father and children. And we know we are going to get what's coming to us—an unbelievable inheritance! We go through exactly what Christ goes through. If we go through the hard times with him, then we're certainly going to go through the good times with him!

KEY PRINCIPLES:

1. **Divine Intervention and Redemption Through Jesus:** The passage highlights the extraordinary way God intervened in human affairs through Jesus Christ. Jesus personally took on human conditions to bring restoration.
2. **The Limitation of the Law:** According to scripture, the law is depicted as inadequate for true healing of human sinfulness. It acted more like a temporary fix rather than a solution to the problem of sin.
3. **Dependence on the Spirit:** Rather than relying on human efforts and becoming obsessed with one's own moral strength, the passage advocates embracing what the Spirit is doing within us. Trusting in God's action leads to spiritual vitality.
4. **The Contrast Between Self-Obsession and God-Focus:** This section contrasts the dead-end of self-obsession with the liberating effect of focusing on God. It argues that focusing on the self leads to a narrow, restricted life. In contrast, focusing on God leads to a spacious and free life.
5. **God's Presence in Believers:** The passage teaches that God takes residence in the lives of those who welcome Him. This dwelling of God's Spirit allows believers to experience life on God's terms, full of life and vitality.

6. **Resurrection Life:** Believers receive a resurrection life from God, which is characterized by adventurous expectancy and childlike trust. It's a life full of hope and aligned with the experiences of Christ.

7. **Relationship between God and Believers:** This section beautifully illustrates the relationship between God and His children, emphasizing the familial relationship between Father and children and the inheritance that awaits them.

8. **Embracing the New Life with God:** The old way of self-reliance is to be abandoned, and believers are to move forward with the new life provided by God's Spirit. This new life beckons with opportunities and adventures in faith.

9. **Suffering and Glory with Christ:** The passage also alludes to the fact that following Christ involves going through both hard times and good times with Him, symbolizing the full range of human experiences.

10. **Confirmation of Identity:** The Spirit touches our spirits, confirming who we really are in relation to God. This affirmation of identity provides assurance, purpose and a sense of belonging.

CONCLUSION:

Today's scripture invites us into a transformative journey that surpasses mere legalism and self-focus, guiding us toward a vibrant relationship with God. At its core, this passage urges us to relinquish our obsession with the superficial and temporary fixes offered by human laws and efforts and instead embrace the profound, life-giving presence of God's Spirit.

Through the powerful imagery of divine intervention, redemption, resurrection and familial relationship, we are reminded that we are not abandoned to our brokenness. God's love reaches us in our most chaotic mess, offering not just a momentary reprieve but a complete renewal and a joyful life in communion with Him. This is not a distant, abstract deity but a Father who calls us children and beckons us to join Him in a dynamic, adventurous life of faith.

The contrasts drawn between self-obsession and God-focus serve as both a warning and an invitation. Where the former leads to a restricted existence, the latter opens up a realm of freedom, love and purpose. This scripture calls us to align ourselves with God's action within us, trusting in His guidance rather than our limited understanding.

In a world that often urges us to rely on our own strength and judgment, this passage provides a refreshing and liberating perspective. It challenges us to reflect on our lives to ask ourselves if we are living a self-centered life or if we are allowing God's Spirit to lead us into the spaciousness of divine love.

It's a reminder that our identity, value and destiny are found not in our fleeting achievements but in our relationship with God, who makes us alive as Christ, confirming who we indeed are.

As we meditate on these holy words, let us be inspired to let go of our old ways, embrace the new life God offers, and walk boldly – hand in hand with our Creator – into the promising future He has promised us. Let us remember that in both the good times and the hard times, we are not alone; we go through them with Christ, and that makes all the difference. It's a calling to a faith that is alive, expectant and eternally connected to the source of all life and love. It's a calling we would do well to heed, for in it lies the path to true freedom and fulfillment.

REFLECTION:

1. In the passage, Jesus' divine intervention is described as Him taking on human conditions to bring restoration, entering the mess of humanity to set it right. Have you ever felt something similar in your life, where a guiding force seemed to intervene in a chaotic situation? Reflect on those experiences and how they may resonate with this understanding of Jesus' guidance and redemption.

2. The passage illustrates the limitation of the law, describing it as a temporary fix rather than a solution to the problem of sin, and it emphasizes Jesus' fulfillment of the law. Consider times when you may have relied on rules or external guidelines to guide your behavior. How did that feel compared to when you acted in alignment with your spiritual beliefs and values? How can people shift from relying on the law to embracing the transformative power of Jesus' intervention instead?

3. In what areas of your life do you find yourself focused more on your desires or image? How might shifting your attention from self to God change your perspective and lead you to a more fulfilling life?

4. We learned that God Himself takes residence in the lives of those who welcome Him, infusing them with life and vitality. How have you personally experienced or felt this presence within yourself? In what ways has this awareness transformed your daily life, actions or decision-making? In moments when you've felt disconnected from Him, consider steps you might take to deepen your connection with God. What steps could you take to allow the Holy Spirit to guide you more fully?

5. you may have faced blessings and trials in your faith journey. The scripture today reminds us that as believers, we share in both Christ's sufferings and His glory, with the assurance that He is with us every step of the way. Reflect on a time when you've experienced hardship in your life. How did the knowledge that Christ was with you impact the experience? How can you lean into this promise during future challenges, knowing that he will never leave you or forsake

you, even during suffering?

6. Have you ever taken a moment to ask God who you really are, what He has called you to be and what your unique purpose is? Reflect on your current path. Are you walking in alignment with this divinely inspired identity and purpose? If not, what might be holding you back? How can the assurance that the Spirit confirms who you really are in relation to God guide you toward a greater sense of purpose and belonging?

7. Reflect on a time when you felt completely reliant on your own strength, abilities or moral judgment. How did that experience feel, and what were the outcomes? Now, think about a time when you fully embraced the Holy Spirit's guidance, surrendering your own efforts to Him. What contrasts do you notice between these two approaches? How can you cultivate a daily practice of depending on the Holy Spirit, and what might that look like in your personal life, relationships and decisions?

PRAYER:

Dear God, I come to You today with a heart full of gratitude for Your presence in my life. Yet, I also recognize the times when I've turned to my own strength, ignoring Your call and guidance. Forgive me, Father, for those moments when I've lost my way.

Your Word today has reminded me of the extraordinary love You have for me, a love that reaches into the very depths of my soul and touches the very core of me. You've shown me the contrast between a life centered on self and a life focused on You. Help me, Lord, to embrace the freedom and joy found in surrendering to Your Spirit.

As I reflect on my journey, I see the blessings and trials that have shaped my faith. Teach me, Father, to recognize Your hand in both, to find Your grace in times of suffering and Your glory in times of joy. Remind me that I am not alone, that You are with me every step of the way.

Lord, reveal to me who I genuinely am in You. Please help me to understand my purpose and to walk boldly in it. Strengthen me to depend on Your Holy Spirit daily and guide my decisions, relationships and actions.

I thank You for the life You have given me, a life full of hope and promise. May I live it fully, with childlike trust and adventurous expectancy, ever looking to You and asking, "What's next, Papa?"

In the powerful and loving name of Jesus Christ, I pray. Amen.

GOING DEEPER:

1. How does the concept of Jesus taking on human conditions to set things right challenge or expand your current understanding of salvation and redemption? Consider writing a personal letter to Jesus, expressing your thoughts and feelings about His divine intervention into humanity.

2. Reflect on the contrast between adhering to a set of rules (the law) and embracing God's unconditional love (grace) as described in Romans 8:3—17. How have these concepts played out in your own life? Think of a situation where mere adherence to rules felt inadequate or limiting, and consider how the application of grace, or a more compassionate and understanding approach, could have transformed that experience.

3. What practical steps can you take to allow the Holy Spirit to fully transform your daily life? How might you structure your day to be more receptive to the Spirit's guidance? What barriers might you need to overcome to do so?

4. Examine areas where self-obsession may overshadow your focus on God. How could you create a plan to redirect that focus and consciously cultivate a God-centered mindset in those specific areas?

5. What does the concept of a resurrection life mean to you personally? Explore how this idea affects your understanding of death, suffering and eternal life. How might this affect the way you approach daily challenges and joys?

6. Think about a time when you clung to the "old way" of self-reliance. What fears or misconceptions were holding you back? Write a letter to your future self, describing the new life you aspire to embrace with God.

7. Reflecting on your personal trials, how have they shaped your faith? Write a prayer or poem that expresses your understanding of suffering and glory as a follower of Christ.

8. In what ways have the opinions or labels from parents, friends or even yourself limited your perception of your true identity? How might these limiting beliefs conflict with what God sees in you and the identity He wants to give you?

9. Have you ever internalized negative comments such as "you're no good" or "you're not good enough" and allowed them to define who you are? How have these thoughts influenced your self-worth and ability to live up to higher potential?

10. What practical steps can you take to retrain your mind, silencing the hurtful noise of the past that may have labeled you? How can you align yourself more closely with God's perception of you, fostering an identity that resonates with faith, love and purpose?

11. Jesus once said, 'Give to Caesar what is Caesar's,' emphasizing the importance of obeying the laws of society. But what happens when these laws or societal norms seem to conflict with God's law or spiritual principles? How can we navigate these complex situations to fulfill our obligations to both earthly authorities and our higher spiritual commitments? In your own life,

can you identify a moment when you faced such a conflict? How did you approach resolving it?

NAVIGATING YOUR JOURNEY:

1. Embrace the transformation. Begin by recognizing the depth of God's love and transformation offered through Christ. Reflect on the changes you might need to move from self-obsession to God-focus, from relying on laws to embracing grace, and from living a restricted existence to an expansive, free life in Christ.

2. Cultivate spiritual dependence. Develop daily practices that allow you to surrender to the Holy Spirit's guidance. This might include regular prayer, meditation on scriptures or seeking spiritual mentorship. Recognize where you might be relying on your strength and seek God's guidance instead.

3. Experience God's presence. Actively seek to feel and acknowledge God's presence in your life. This can include intentional times of worship, participation in a faith community or practicing mindfulness to God's constant presence throughout the day.

4. Align with your divine purpose. Spend time in prayer and reflection to understand God's unique calling for your life. Consider journaling or seeking spiritual counsel to clarify and align your path with this divinely inspired purpose.

5. Navigate through trials with Christ. Recognize that hardships are a part of the Christian journey, but they are not faced alone. In times of suffering, lean on the promise that Christ is with you. Seek support from a faith community and remember to look for God's grace in both good times and hard times.

6. Build a resurrection mindset. Embrace the concept of a resurrection life filled with hope, adventurous expectancy and childlike trust. Let this mindset influence your daily choices, leading you to a life filled with joy and connection to Christ.

7. Share your journey. Your personal experiences of divine intervention, redemption, transformation and relationship with God are not only for you but are part of your testimony to share with others. Consider how you might encourage or guide others in their faith journey, using your story to illustrate God's love and power.

By applying these principles and actively seeking to navigate your life according to God's guidance, you can live a life that transcends mere rules and self-focus and embodies the rich, fulfilling relationship God offers through Christ. It's a path that leads to true freedom and fulfillment, one step at a time, hand in hand with your Creator.

Remember, the journey is not about perfection but progression. It's about moving closer to God and becoming more like Christ every day. Be patient with yourself and trust in God's timing and direction. The path might not always be easy, but with God's love and guidance, you are never alone.

Day 26: The Eternal Covenant: Remembrance, Revelation and Worship

---

FOCUS:

Gratitude

SONG:

When I Think About Jesus – Kirk Franklin & The Family

INTRODUCTION:

AS WE ENGAGE WITH 1 Chronicles 16:7-19, let's contemplate how gratitude and acknowledgment of God's unchanging commitments can help us to better understand His guidance in our lives and the inheritance He promises. By doing so, we open ourselves to a deeper, more meaningful relationship with him. It is through this constant recognition of God's hand that deep-seated gratitude can truly take root within us.

READING:

1 Chronicles 16:7-19a (MSG)

That was the day that David inaugurated regular worship of praise to God, led by Asaph and his company. Thank God! Call out his Name! Tell the world who he is and what he's done! Sing to him! Play songs for him! Broadcast all his wonders! Revel in his holy Name, God-seekers, be jubilant! Study God and his strength, seek his presence day and night; Remember all the wonders he performed, the miracles and judgments that came out of his mouth. Seed of Israel his servant! Children of Jacob, his first choice! He is God, our God; wherever you go, you come on his judgments and decisions. He keeps his commitments across thousands of generations, the covenant he commanded, The same one he made with Abraham, the very one he swore to Isaac; He posted it in big block letters to Jacob, this eternal covenant with Israel: 'I give you the land of Canaan, this is your inheritance.

KEY PRINCIPLES:

1. **Gratitude and Praise:** The passage begins with the inauguration of regular worship of praise to God. This sets a standard for the importance of constant gratitude and celebration of God's deeds. It's a personal acknowledgment and a call to proclaim His greatness to the world.

2. **Seeking God Continuously:** The urging to "seek His presence day and night" emphasizes the constant need for a relationship with God. It's not a part-time endeavor but a full-time commitment to study, seek and revel in His presence.

3. **Remembering God's Wonders:** Recalling the wonders, miracles and judgments performed by God helps reinforce faith and trust in Him. Remembering what God has done in the past can encourage us in the present and future.

4. **God's unchanging Commitment:** The reference to God's covenant that spans thousands of generations, from Abraham to Isaac and Jacob, highlights God's unwavering promise and commitment. This eternal covenant is not just a historical fact but a living truth that speaks to His faithfulness.

5. **God as the Source of Guidance and Judgment:** The phrase "wherever you go, you come on his judgments and decisions" portrays God as the ultimate source of wisdom, guidance and judgment. His sovereignty is beyond our immediate understanding, and His ways are to be respected and followed.

6. **Inheritance and Promise:** The promise of the land of Canaan as an inheritance is symbolic of God's provision and blessing. It serves as a tangible representation of the spiritual inheritance believers receive from God.

7. **Unity in Worship:** The passage also shows unity in worship, led by Asaph and his company. Worship is not only an individual act but a communal experience where believers come together to glorify God.

8. **Exuberant Celebration of God's Nature:** Through songs, reveling in His name and broadcasting His wonders, there is an expression of joy and exuberance in recognizing God's nature. It's not a solemn, detached observation but an engaged, joyful participation in recognizing who God is.

CONCLUSION:

1 Chronicles 16:7-19 paints a vivid picture of celebration of God's nature and His enduring promises. It's not just a historical account but a living call to action. The scripture encourages us to transcend mere acknowledgment and to embrace an engaged, jubilant relationship with God.

The praise and gratitude expressed are not confined to a particular moment or place but are interwoven into daily living, urging us to seek His presence continually. These verses remind us of God's unchanging commitment, one that stretches beyond time, resonating with us today as it did with Abraham, Isaac and Jacob. The promise of inheritance isn't merely a physical gift but a wonderful spiritual blessing that God bestows upon those who follow Him.

We are called to remember the wonders He has performed, not just with our minds but with our hearts. We learn that God's presence isn't a remote or abstract concept but a tangible reality that informs our judgments, decisions and daily lives. It's a call to community, unity in worship and an exuberant celebration of God's nature. The scripture doesn't merely narrate; it inspires and invites us into a dynamic dance of faith.

REFLECTION:

1. Reveling in God's name means to take immense pleasure and joy in recognizing His character, celebrating His goodness and delighting in His love. Have there been moments in your life where you've praised or celebrated God so passionately that it surprised even you? How could you encourage yourself to take this joyful and exuberant recognition into your daily life, telling others about His goodness and love or expressing it through songs, dance or other creative expressions? What specific actions could help you grow in this engaged, joyful participation with God?
2. How can you make a conscious effort to celebrate and acknowledge His deeds not only privately but also publicly?
3. The land of Canaan is often symbolic of the promises and blessings that God bestows, representing a place of abundance, provision and rest. How do you perceive the spiritual inheritance that God promises? What does the land of Canaan mean to you in light of this understanding? How does it reflect your thoughts on God's provision and blessing?
4. Think about a time when you witnessed or felt God's wonders, miracles or judgments. What effect did this experience have on you? How can you keep that memory alive?
5. A covenant is a binding agreement between two parties, often solemn and sacred. In the context of the Bible, God's covenants with His people represent His unbreakable promises

and steadfast love. These covenants remind us of God's faithfulness, unchanging nature, and eternal commitment to those who follow Him. For example, as mentioned in today's study, God's covenant with Abraham, Isaac and Jacob illustrates His promise to be their God and bless them and their descendants. With this understanding in mind:

    a. How do you view God's covenants, and what do they signify to you in your relationship with Him?

    b. Can you recall a specific instance when you felt the reassurance of God's unchanging commitment in your life? How did it affect your trust in Him?

    c. How can you daily live in the assurance of God's covenants, allowing them to shape your decisions, faith and connection to God?

6. Being in a relationship with God is akin to a dynamic dance of faith. Have you ever felt like you were in step with God, following His lead in a particular situation or decision? What was that like, and how did it feel? In what ways have you experienced the joy, freedom or creativity that can be likened to dancing in your relationship with God?

7. Are there areas in your life where you might feel out of step with God's rhythm? What steps can you take to get back in sync?

8. How can you cultivate a daily practice that keeps you attuned to God's leading, allowing your life to be a vibrant dance of faith and trust in Him?

PRAYER:

DEAR GOD, AS I COME before You today, my heart is filled with gratitude and wonder at Your unwavering commitment to me. The lessons in Your Word, the joyous praises sung to You and the images of a dynamic dance of faith all strike a chord within me, reminding me of Your presence in my life.

I am in awe of Your eternal covenant, the promises that span generations, reaching even to me. How can I ever doubt Your faithfulness when You've shown time and again that Your love never fails? Teach me to revel in Your name, to take pleasure in knowing You more and to dance in harmony with Your will.

The land of Canaan, a symbol of Your blessing and provision, stirs in me a longing for all that You have prepared for me. Help me to walk in the path You've laid out, trusting that You lead me to places of abundance and rest.

I thank you for the community of believers, for unity in worship, for songs that lift Your name high. May my life be a joyful celebration of who You are, not just in the grand moments but in the daily, intimate dance with You.

Lord, if there are areas where I'm out of step with Your rhythm, guide me back into sync. Help me to remember Your wonders, to keep the memories alive in my heart and to lean on Your unchanging commitment.

I pray that my life reflects a deep-seated gratitude, not just with words but in action, love, and faith. You've called me into a relationship with You that's as beautiful and engaging as a dance, and I want to move to Your beat, fully engaged in this wonderful journey with You.

Thank You for being my Guide, Provider and Eternal Partner in this dance of life. I love You, Lord, and commit myself anew to follow Your lead.

In Jesus' name, I pray. Amen.

GOING DEEPER:

1. Gratitude often involves recognizing the good, even in challenging circumstances. How can you practice seeing God's grace and blessings in times of personal difficulty or societal unrest? What specific steps can you take to cultivate a more profound sense of gratitude during these times?

2. In community worship, believers often come together to celebrate God. How can you take an active role in fostering a community where praises, testimonies and shared experiences are regularly expressed? What might be the impact on those who are new to the faith or struggling with their beliefs?

3. David and the Israelites praised God in community, sharing their recognition of His wondrous deeds together. How might communal expressions of gratitude, such as sharing testimonies, strengthen not only your personal faith but also your church or faith community?

4. Reflecting on God's faithfulness across generations can bring revealing insights. Have you ever explored your family or cultural heritage to uncover stories or traditions that highlight God's guidance? How do these historical connections inform your current relationship with God and gratitude toward Him? How might the practice of remembrance, such as keeping a journal or another record of God's faithfulness to you or others in your family, deepen your sense of thankfulness and perhaps affect generations who come after you?

5. How can you make the act of remembering God's works a daily spiritual practice rather than a sporadic event? Consider creative ways, such as art, poetry or music to document God's faithfulness. How might these practices enrich your spiritual life and your connection to the community?

6. Have you ever faced a situation where gratitude seemed impossible or where you felt out of step with God's plan? Reflect on that experience and consider what resources, practices, or relationships helped you realign with God's rhythm. How can you apply these insights to future challenges in your journey?

7. The land of Canaan symbolizes God's promises and blessings. How do you understand and relate to God's promises in a world that often seems uncertain and ever-changing? How can you anchor your faith in God's unchanging nature while navigating the complexities of modern life?

8. The metaphor of a "dynamic dance of faith" presents an image of a faith that is alive, active and constantly moving. Unlike more static or traditional metaphors that might depict faith as a solid rock or a firm foundation, dance is something that is fluid, expressive and requires engagement and participation. What does this metaphor reveal about the nature of faith that more traditional images might not capture? How can you embrace this dynamic, flexible and creative approach in your daily walk with the Lord?

NAVIGATING YOUR JOURNEY:

1. Embrace daily gratitude. Create a gratitude journal where you write down daily blessings, no matter how big or small. This practice can cultivate a continual awareness of God's presence and provision in your life.

2. Engage in communal worship. Participate actively in your community's worship services and gatherings. Share testimonies, praises or simply be present with others. The shared experience can deepen your connection to God and fellow believers.

3. Dance with God. Take time to reflect on what it means to be in a "dynamic dance of faith" with God. Perhaps literally put on some music and dance, considering how you can move in harmony with God's will in your daily life.

4. Explore your spiritual inheritance. Reflect on what the promises and blessings of God mean to you. Engage with the symbols and metaphors like the land of Canaan in your meditation or prayer, asking God to reveal the specific meaning for your life.

5. Remember and record God's faithfulness. Keep a record of God's wondrous deeds in your life. This could be a journal, art or even a shared family document that captures the faith journey across generations.

6. Seek alignment with God's rhythm. Identify areas where you might feel out of step with God and seek guidance through prayer, scripture or conversation with mentors to get back in sync.

7. Extend gratitude to others. Practicing gratitude isn't only about recognizing God's blessings. It also involves expressing appreciation to others around you. Send a thank-you note, verbalize your appreciation or perform an act of kindness.

THE JOURNEY OF FAITH is rich, dynamic and full of joyous celebration. By embracing practices that foster gratitude, connection and alignment with God's will, you can transform your daily walk into a lively and expressive dance with the Divine. Embracing this dance invites a deeper connection with God and the community of faith around you, as you navigate the ever-changing rhythms of life with joy and gratitude.

Day 27: Seizing Every Opportunity with Insight and Purpose

FOCUS:

Wisdom

SONG:

More Than Able – Elevation Worship

INTRODUCTION:

THIS PASSAGE OFFERS us a chance to reflect on the kind of life we choose to lead, the significance of considering wisdom as not merely a concept but a practical principle, and its role in our daily decisions. We are called to live life with intentionality.

READING:

Ephesians 5:15-17 (NIV)

Be very careful, then, how you live—not as unwise but as wise, making the most of every opportunity, because the days are evil. Therefore do not be foolish, but understand what the Lord's will is.

KEY PRINCIPLES:

1. **Intentional Living:** The passage begins with an explicit instruction to be careful and intentional about how we live. It's not just about avoiding unwise decisions but actively choosing wisdom in all things.

2. **Wisdom as a Choice:** Wisdom is not presented as something that merely happens to us; it's a deliberate choice. We are called to live not as unwise but as wise, suggesting that wisdom should be actively pursued and applied.

3. **Making the Most of Every Opportunity:** The text encourages us to seize opportunities and make the most of our time. It's a call to be proactive and not passive in our approach to life, recognizing the value of each moment.

4. **Understanding the Lord's Will:** The passage emphasizes the importance of discerning and understanding God's will for our lives. This understanding guides our decisions and aligns our lives with God's purposes.

5. **Avoidance of Foolishness:** This is the flip side of seeking wisdom. The passage warns against foolishness, indicating that there is a clear difference between wise living and foolish living, and the choices we make have significant consequences.

6. **Responsiveness to the Times:** The phrase "because the days are evil" highlights the need to be responsive to the times and circumstances we find ourselves in. It's a call to be aware of the world around us and to live wisely in response to the challenges and opportunities presented.

7. **Alignment with Divine Principles:** By seeking wisdom and understanding the Lord's will, we align ourselves with divine principles. This alignment leads to a life that is fulfilling and in harmony with God's design and desires for us.

CONCLUSION:

Ephesians 5:15-17's exhortation calls us to live our lives with intention and wisdom. It's not just a simple encouragement but a deliberate invitation to choose a path of wisdom, making the most of every moment in alignment with the Lord's will. This wisdom isn't an abstract or theoretical concept but a practical, day-to-day guide that shapes our decisions, attitudes and reactions to the world.

The warning against foolishness, paired with the instruction to understand God's will, creates a dual emphasis on both what to avoid and what to seek. It's not enough to simply refrain from foolishness; we must actively pursue wisdom. In a chaotic and overwhelming world, this wisdom provides a firm grounding, helping us navigate life's challenges with grace and insight.

One cannot ignore the urgent tone of the passage, especially the reference to "evil days." It's a reminder to remain vigilant, aware of the times, and aligned with divine principles even in the face of adversity. It's not merely a lesson for the ancient Ephesians but a timeless teaching that continues to have an impact, offering guidance and encouragement as we strive to live wisely in our own times.

REFLECTION:

1. Ephesians 5:15 tells us to "be very careful" in how we live. In the original Greek text, the word translated as "careful" is represented by Strong's Concordance number G199, meaning to live diligently, perfectly or circumspectly. (Strong's Concordance is a reference tool that links words in the Bible back to their original languages.) "Diligent" typically refers to careful and persistent effort or work. What does living diligently mean to you personally? How does this translate into your daily life, and where might you strive to be more diligent?

2. The same Greek word, Strong's G199, also means living perfectly or completely. In a spiritual context, perfection often doesn't mean being without fault but rather being complete or whole, striving toward the fullness of character that God desires for us. How do you interpret the idea of living a "whole" or "perfect" life in alignment with divine principles? What steps are you currently taking, or could you take, to strive for this completeness in your relationship with God and your daily decisions?

3. The verses encourage us to live not as unwise but as wise, actively choosing a path of wisdom. How often do you find yourself on "autopilot," reacting to life rather than consciously making choices? What steps can you take to become more aware and intentional in your daily decisions?

4. Making decisions that reflect a deep understanding of our purpose and God's plan requires attentiveness and active engagement. How can you better align your daily decisions with divine principles? When making decisions, how often do you consider them through the lens of the Bible? What might help you keep this focus throughout the day so that your choices become more deliberate and aligned with His will?

5. Being a passive participant in life can lead to missed opportunities and a lack of fulfillment. How can you take a more assertive role in your life, actively choosing wisdom and intentionality? What barriers or challenges might you need to overcome to live more purposefully?

6. In Ephesians 5:16, the phrase "because the days are evil" highlights the need to be aware of the world around us and to live wisely in response to the challenges and opportunities presented. Given the many incidents in the world that might be seen as evidence of these "evil days," what are some things you've personally seen or heard about?

7. How do you wisely respond to these challenges? Do you bury your head in the sand, react violently, stand for righteousness and justice or perhaps long for the "good old days and ways of life" that may have been "good" for some but not others? How can you take a more intentional and compassionate approach, informed by wisdom and understanding, to engage with the world in ways that reflect the love and justice of God?

8. Can you think of a time when you missed an opportunity you later realized was significant? What did you learn from that experience? How has it informed your approach to recognizing and embracing opportunities now?

9. How can you not only make the most of opportunities for yourself but also create or facilitate opportunities for others? How might your actions open doors for those around you, particularly those with fewer chances?

PRAYER:

Heavenly Father, I come before you with a heart filled with gratitude for Your guidance and wisdom. I recognize that the path before me is filled with choices, and I desire to walk with intentionality, not just reacting to life but consciously choosing the path You've set before me.

Lord, I admit there are times when I have been on autopilot, missing opportunities and failing to live with the diligence You call me to. Forgive me for those moments and awaken my heart to the reality of each precious moment, to seize them with a purpose aligned with Your will.

Your Word reminds me that wisdom is not something that merely happens to us; it is a choice, a pursuit. Please help me to choose wisdom in all things. Grant me discernment to recognize opportunities to grow, to serve and to reflect Your love.

I pray for the strength to stand firm in righteousness and justice, even in the face of the chaos and challenges of these times. Teach me to respond not with violence or indifference but with the wisdom and compassion that reflect Your heart.

Lord, open my eyes to see the doors You've opened for me and grant me the courage to walk through them. Help me also to facilitate opportunities for others, reflecting Your generosity and love.

Above all, guide me to a deeper understanding of Your will for my life so that I may live in alignment with Your divine principles. Let my life be not just a series of accidental events but a meaningful journey guided by Your hand.

Thank you, Lord, for Your faithfulness, wisdom, and endless love. I trust in You and commit my life to walking in Your wisdom, seizing every opportunity for Your glory.

In Jesus' name, I pray. Amen.

GOING DEEPER:

1. Understanding why an unwise choice feels right at the time requires honest self-reflection. It involves examining emotions, beliefs, pressures and values at play in that moment. It may also include acknowledging personal weaknesses or potential growth areas, such as impulsiveness, a desire to please others or prioritization of short-term gains over long-term wisdom. That being said,
    a. Can you recall an unwise decision you made? What factors contributed to that choice at the time? How did you feel afterward?
    b. How did you navigate the consequences of that unwise choice? What support systems did you rely on? What spiritual principles guided your response?
    c. How has your understanding of wisdom evolved through your experiences with unwise choices? How do you now define and pursue wisdom in your daily life?
    d. How can you help others struggling with the consequences of unwise choices? How might our experiences and insights offer support or guidance to them?
2. How do you perceive different levels of foolishness, ranging from seemingly "innocent" acts like pranks to more serious misbehaviors like online harassment? How do these levels impact your understanding of what constitutes wise living?
3. How does anonymity, particularly online, contribute to behaviors considered foolish or even vile? Have you ever encountered or observed this in your online interactions? How do you navigate this environment while maintaining integrity and wisdom?
4. How does the anonymity provided by online platforms sometimes foster a false sense of boldness, enabling individuals to say or do things they wouldn't dare do if identified? Why might someone feel empowered to act in ways that conflict with wisdom and integrity when hidden behind a screen? How does this align or conflict with the biblical warning against foolishness?
5. Given the potential for anonymity to lead to unwise or harmful actions, how can you ensure that you maintain wisdom and integrity in your online interactions? What strategies might you employ to challenge or respond to unwise or unkind behavior online? How can you model responsible conduct in a way that aligns with biblical principles?
6. What role do forgiveness, self-reflection and growth play in moving beyond foolish choices?
7. How have you observed or experienced situations where affiliations, such as political parties or social groups, have been prioritized above what is right and just according to God's holy word? In what ways can this lead to a perversion of scripture, bending it to our will instead of aligning

our will with God's? How can this result in accepting behavior that might be unacceptable within a biblical context?

8. Reflect on when you might have been tempted to put your affiliations above divine principles. What steps can you take to ensure our beliefs and actions align with scripture rather than bending it to fit personal or group biases? How can you foster a commitment to seeking God's will, even when it may conflict with societal pressures or affiliations?

NAVIGATING YOUR JOURNEY:

1. Embrace intentionality. Start each day with a conscious decision to live wisely. Reflect on your goals, align them with divine principles and set deliberate intentions to guide your thoughts and actions.

2. Develop self-awareness. Regularly evaluate your choices and actions. Identify areas where you may act out of impulse or societal pressures and strive to align more closely with wisdom and integrity.

3. Seek Opportunities. Be proactive in identifying and seizing opportunities that align with God's will and your purpose. Whether in personal growth, serving others or professional endeavors, make the most of every moment.

4. Foster digital responsibility. Commit to responsible online behavior. Recognize the false boldness that anonymity might foster and pledge to uphold wisdom and integrity in all your interactions, even when anonymous.

5. Invest in relationships. Surround yourself with people who share your values and can hold you accountable. These relationships can be a source of encouragement, guidance and wisdom.

6. Grow in understanding of God's will. Engage in continuous study, prayer and reflection to deepen your understanding of God's plan for your life. Seek guidance from mentors, pastors or trusted friends who can provide insight into divine principles.

7. Practice forgiveness and compassion. Embrace a compassionate approach toward yourself and others. Acknowledge mistakes, learn from them and extend forgiveness where needed, recognizing it as a pathway to growth and wisdom.

8. Evaluate our affiliations. Regularly examine your affiliations and the groups you are part of, whether political, social or otherwise. Consider if they align with your spiritual beliefs and God's word. Be willing to make tough choices to prioritize what is right and just according to divine principles over societal or group pressures.

9. Cultivate spiritual discernment. Foster a commitment to seeking God's will, even when it may conflict with societal norms or affiliations. Engage in continuous prayer, seeking wisdom and guidance from mentors and spiritual leaders. Be open to self-correction and growth, aligning

your beliefs and actions with Scripture rather than bending it to fit personal or group biases. Make a conscious effort to base decisions on biblical principles and seek accountability from those who share your faith.

Embarking on this journey is about more than personal growth; it's a conscious commitment to aligning every aspect of life with divine principles, nurturing relationships and living with integrity in both digital and physical realms. It's a continuous process of seeking wisdom, making intentional choices and holding oneself accountable, all while navigating the complex landscape of modern life through a lens of faith and spiritual discernment.

Day 28: Navigating Challenges: Empowered and Guided by the Comforter (The Spirit of Truth)

FOCUS:

Guidance

SONG:

Stand - Donnie McClurkin

INTRODUCTION:

IN JOHN 16:1-15, JESUS prepares His disciples for the trials ahead, telling them about the persecution they will face. However, He assures them of the coming Helper, the Holy Spirit, who will guide them in truth and help them make sense of Jesus' teachings. This promise of divine guidance is not limited to the disciples but extends to us as well, offering assurance as we navigate the complexities of life.

READING:

John 16:1-15 (MSG)

I've told you these things to prepare you for rough times ahead. They are going to throw you out of the meeting places. There will even come a time when anyone who kills you will think he's doing God a favor. They will do these things because they never really understood the Father. I've told you these things so that when the time comes and they start in on you, you'll be well-warned and ready for them.

I didn't tell you this earlier because I was with you every day. But now I am on my way to the One who sent me. Not one of you has asked, 'Where are you going?' Instead, the longer I've talked, the sadder you've become. So let me say it again, this truth: It's better for you that I leave. If I don't leave, the Friend won't come. But if I go, I'll send him to you.

When he comes, he'll expose the error of the godless world's view of sin, righteousness, and judgment: He'll show them that their refusal to believe in me is their basic sin; that righteousness comes from above, where I am with the Father, out of their sight and control; that judgment takes place as the ruler of this godless world is brought to trial and convicted.

I still have many things to tell you, but you can't handle them now. But when the Friend comes, the Spirit of the Truth, he will take you by the hand and guide you into all the truth there is. He won't draw attention to himself, but will make sense out of what is about to happen and, indeed, of all that I have done and said. He will honor me; he will take from me and deliver it to you. Everything the Father has is also mine. That is why I've said, 'He takes from me and delivers to you.'

BEYOND DEVOTIONALS: A 31-DAY DEEP DIVE INTO ALIGNING WITH GOD'S WILL

KEY PRINCIPLES:

1. **Preparation for Persecution:** Jesus is preparing His followers for their challenges and persecutions, emphasizing the importance of being well-warned and ready.
2. **The Promise of the Holy Spirit:** Jesus promises the coming of the Holy Spirit, the "Helper" or "Friend," who will guide believers into all truth, making sense of Jesus' teachings and acting as a continual presence in their lives.
3. **Exposure of Sin and Righteousness:** The Holy Spirit will expose the world's misconceptions about sin, righteousness and judgment, highlighting the refusal to believe in Jesus as a fundamental error.
4. **Connection to the Divine:** The Holy Spirit acts as an intermediary, taking what belongs to Jesus and the Father and delivering it to believers. This offers a continuous connection to divine wisdom and guidance, and it emphasizes Jesus' oneness with the Father.
5. **Guidance into Truth:** The Holy Spirit will not draw attention to Himself but will guide believers into all the truth, helping them to understand not just the events that are about to unfold but also the entirety of Jesus' teachings.
6. **Judgment of the Godless World:** There is an underlying theme of judgment, where the ruler of the godless world will be brought to trial and convicted, showing a divine plan that moves toward justice and righteousness.

CONCLUSION:

In this passage, Jesus prepares us for the inevitable challenges and trials that lie ahead, painting a realistic picture of a world that may not always align with God's principles. But He doesn't leave us to face these struggles alone. He promises the guidance of the Holy Spirit, a Helper who will lead us into all truth, making sense of complex teachings and worldly dilemmas.

This assurance offers more than mere comfort; it's a call to a deeper, more meaningful relationship with God. It's an invitation to grow in our understanding, wrestle with challenging ideas, and emerge with a robust and resilient faith.

Jesus' words encourage us to confidently lean into our spiritual journey, knowing that the Holy Spirit is our constant companion. Even in the face of misunderstanding or opposition, we are called to a path of righteousness and truth. This scripture serves as a timeless reminder that we are never alone in our journey, and the wisdom and strength we seek are always within our reach, guided by the supportive hand that equips us with all that we need.

REFLECTION:

1. The Holy Spirit has been described in various roles, such as helper, friend, comforter, counselor, intercessor, and revealer of truth. Can you recall specific moments in your life when you experienced the Holy Spirit's presence in one or more of these roles? How did those moments unfold, and how did they make you feel? Whether you reached out to the Holy Spirit yourself or someone did so on your behalf, what lasting impact did those experiences have on your life?

2. Reflecting on Jesus' assurance of the Holy Spirit guiding us into all truth, in what situations have you felt a strong sense of guidance or clarity that you believe came from the Holy Spirit? How did that guidance align with your understanding of truth, and how did it impact your decision-making?

3. Jesus warns His followers of trials and tribulations they might face. Can you identify a moment when you faced adversity or misunderstanding due to your faith? How did you navigate that situation? Did you feel the presence of the Holy Spirit during that time?

4. The Holy Spirit is described as honoring Jesus by taking from Him and delivering to us. Have there been moments when you've felt particularly close to the teachings of Christ, possibly even feeling a direct connection or revelation? Like, "A-ha! This is an on-time message." Or just a feeling that the pastor's lesson was written precisely for what you're going through at the time. How did these moments shape your relationship with God?

5. Jesus speaks of the Spirit's role in exposing error and guiding judgment. How have you engaged with discernment in your own life? Can you recall when you felt the Holy Spirit assisting you in distinguishing right from wrong? What were the outcomes of those insights?

6. Jesus also mentioned that the Holy Spirit will not draw attention to Himself but will make sense out of what is about to happen. Have you experienced a time when things seemed confusing or overwhelming, and then clarity emerged, perhaps in a way that felt beyond your understanding? How did that experience influence your trust in the guidance of the Holy Spirit?

7. God's righteousness is a moral and ethical standard that is pure, unchanging and aligned with His perfect character. It is a call to live in accordance with His will, as revealed in the Scriptures, and is often characterized by love, justice, mercy and humility. In contrast, human concepts of righteousness can be tainted by personal biases, cultural influences or self-serving motives, leading to a distorted or incomplete understanding of what it truly means to be righteous.

    a. Think about a time when you had to choose between doing what everyone else thought was right and what you believed God wanted you to do. How did you figure out the right thing to do?

    b. What did you learn from that experience? How has it helped you make choices in your life?

PRAYER:

FATHER, IN A WORLD filled with confusion, conflicting opinions and a maze of rights and wrongs, I turn to You, seeking Your truth and guidance. You have promised the Holy Spirit to be my Helper, my Guide and my Comforter, and I humbly ask to feel His presence more clearly and more deeply in my daily walk.

I confess that there have been times when I've been led astray by my own understanding or the voices around me. Forgive me for those moments when I failed to seek Your guidance and chose my path. Thank You for always being there, ready to lead me back to Your righteousness.

Help me to be attentive to the voice of the Holy Spirit, to recognize Your truth amid the noise and to stand firm even when it's not popular or easy. Empower me to be a beacon of Your love and justice, reflecting Your character in all I say and do.

Thank You, Lord, for the assurance that you are with me even in the roughest times. I'm never alone, and I have a Friend who understands my struggles, celebrates my victories and guides me through every challenge. May I always lean on You, trusting that Your wisdom and strength are always within my reach.

In Jesus's name, I pray. Amen.

GOING DEEPER:

1. If God's way of doing what's right is always the same and completely pure, why do you think it's sometimes hard for people to see it clearly? Could personal opinions or the way society thinks be getting in the way? How so? How can you recognize God's true righteousness in your own life?

2. The Holy Spirit is described as not drawing attention to Himself but guiding us into all truth. In a world that often equates loudness with authority and correctness, how can you cultivate a sensitive heart that recognizes the subtle nudges and whispers of the Holy Spirit? What might you need to let go of to hear Him more clearly? What voices in society (political, religious,

or even your friends and family) seem loud and speak with authority but may be the opposite of what the Holy Spirit considers truth and righteousness? Are you ready to walk away from those voices? Why or why not?

3. How would you handle a situation where standing for your faith might lead to severe consequences like losing friendships, opportunities or even personal safety? Have you thought about the practicalities of what it means to live a life fully aligned with Christ's teachings, even when it's countercultural or risky?

4. The passage speaks about judgment, conviction and exposing error. How do you balance the call to live righteously and the command to love others, especially those with different beliefs or values? How can you approach judgment in a way that reflects God's character rather than human anger or self-righteousness?

5. If the Holy Spirit has so many roles – Helper, Friend, Comforter, Counselor, Intercessor, Revealer of Truth, etc. – why do you think many believers only experience Him in limited ways? How might your relationship with God change if you were to seek and embrace the fullness of the Holy Spirit's work in your life?

6. Jesus promises that the Holy Spirit will make sense out of what is about to happen, even when it seems confusing or overwhelming. How do you develop a faith that doesn't just survive but thrives amid uncertainties and complexities? How can you actively build a robust and resilient trust, deeply rooted in Christ's teachings and not swayed or easily influenced by different opinions ideas or false teachings?

7. How do you think we gain understanding from the Holy Spirit about Jesus' teachings? Do you think we need to ask for it specifically, or does it come naturally as we read and experience His words? How have you personally felt the Holy Spirit guiding your understanding of the Bible?

8. How have you seen human judgments fall short or cause harm? What lessons can be learned from reflecting on the differences between human and divine judgment? How can these insights shape how you engage with others, especially those with whom you disagree?

NAVIGATING YOUR JOURNEY:

1. Stay grounded in scripture. Make regular reading and meditation on the Bible a priority. Understanding the teachings of Jesus is essential for discerning God's will and recognizing the guidance of the Holy Spirit.

2. Seek the Holy Spirit's guidance. Don't hesitate to ask for the Holy Spirit's guidance through prayer. Whether facing a difficult decision or seeking clarity on a spiritual matter, turn to the

Holy Spirit for insight and direction.

3. Build resilient faith. Cultivate a faith that thrives by surrounding yourself with a supportive spiritual community. Engage in personal reflection, worship and fellowship to strengthen your relationship with God.

4. Practice discernment. Learn to recognize and differentiate between personal biases, cultural influences and God's righteousness. Prayerfully consider your actions and attitudes to align them with Christ's teachings.

5. Embrace the fullness of the Holy Spirit. Acknowledge and explore the various roles of the Holy Spirit in your life. Whether as Comforter, Counselor, Guide or something else, seek to experience all that the Holy Spirit has to offer.

6. Prepare for challenges. Understand that living a Christ-centered life may lead to misunderstandings or opposition. Strengthen yourself through prayer, study and fellowship so that you can stand firm in your faith, even during trials.

7. Show love and compassion. Balance your pursuit of righteousness with a loving attitude toward others. Reflect Christ's love and grace in your interactions even in disagreements or judgments.

8. Reflect and grow. Regularly take time to reflect on your experiences with the Holy Spirit and the teachings of Jesus. Acknowledge growth, identify areas for improvement and celebrate victories in your spiritual journey.

DEALING WITH THE COMPLEXITIES of faith is an ongoing journey filled with growth opportunities, understanding and deepening connections with God. By embracing the guidance of the Holy Spirit, staying rooted in Christ's teachings and fostering resilience, you can confidently traverse the path of righteousness. Remember, you are never alone on this journey, and the wisdom and strength you seek are always within reach, guided by the loving hand that equips you with all that you need.

Day 29: Living in Abundant Love: Gratitude, Prayer and Sharing God's Goodness

---

FOCUS:

Gratitude

SONG:

I Will Bless The Lord – Byron Cage

INTRODUCTION:

IN PHILIPPIANS 1:2-11, Paul expresses his heartfelt affection and gratitude for the believers of Philippi. He celebrates their partnership in the gospel, their faithfulness through trials, and their shared experience of God's generous help. At the core of Paul's message is his prayer for their love to grow and flourish – a love that is sincere, discerning, and action-oriented. Paul's message is an encouragement for us today, a call to live lives marked by love, wisdom and faithfulness, ultimately making Jesus Christ attractive to all.

READING:

Philippians 1:2-11 (MSG)

We greet you with the grace and peace that comes from God our Father and our Master, Jesus Christ. Every time you cross my mind, I break out in exclamations of thanks to God. Each exclamation is a trigger to prayer. I find myself praying for you with a glad heart. I am so pleased that you have continued on in this with us, believing and proclaiming God's Message, from the day you heard it right up to the present. There has never been the slightest doubt in my mind that the God who started this great work in you would keep at it and bring it to a flourishing finish on the very day Christ Jesus appears.

It is not at all fanciful for me to think this way about you. My prayers and hopes have deep roots in reality. You have, after all, stuck with me all the way from the time I was thrown in jail, put on trial, and came out of it in one piece. All along you have experienced with me the most generous help from God. He knows how much I love and miss you these days. Sometimes I think I feel as strongly about you as Christ does!

So this is my prayer: that your love will flourish and that you will not only love much but well. Learn to love appropriately. You need to use your head and test your feelings so that your love is sincere and intelligent, not sentimental gush. Live a lover's life, circumspect and exemplary, a life Jesus will be proud of: bountiful in fruits from the soul, making Jesus Christ attractive to all, getting everyone involved in the glory and praise of God.

KEY PRINCIPLES:

1. **Gratitude and Prayer:** Paul's consistent gratitude for the Philippians makes him pray for them regularly. His grateful heart is a model for all believers, showing the importance of acknowledging and giving thanks for the people and blessings in our lives.
2. **Partnership in the Gospel:** The believers in Philippi were partners with Paul in spreading the Gospel. This shows the importance of working together in community and unity, recognizing that the mission of spreading the faith is a shared responsibility.
3. **Faithfulness Through Trials:** Paul emphasizes the believers' steadfast faith, even during trials and difficulties. This principle underscores the importance of remaining faithful to God's calling and purpose, regardless of the circumstances.
4. **God's Faithful Work:** The confidence that God, who began a good work in believers, will carry it to completion is central to the text. This speaks to the assurance of God's faithfulness and providence in guiding and sustaining His people.
5. **Love That is Discerning and Action-Oriented:** Paul's prayer for the Philippians is that their love grows in sincerity and intelligence. He urges them to love well, not just much. This emphasizes the need for discernment, wisdom and action in love, rather than mere sentimentality.
6. **Hope and Assurance in Christ's Return:** The passage alludes to the future return of Christ and the completion of the work He has begun in believers. This provides a hope and assurance that gives perspective and meaning to the daily walk of faith.

CONCLUSION:

The passage from Philippians 1:2-11 is not just a letter from Paul to a specific community; it's a timeless message that resonates with believers today. At its heart, it's an invitation to a life marked by gratitude, discerning love and steadfast faithfulness.

Gratitude here isn't just a fleeting emotion; it's an acknowledgment of God's presence and the connections we forge with one another. It leads to a prayerful life where thanks transform into action and action into a partnership for a higher calling.

The love that Paul prays for us is not mere sentimentality; it's an intelligent, sincere love that knows when and how to act. It's a love guided by wisdom, committed to making our feelings and our entire lives a reflection of Christ's teachings.

Amidst trials, the believers in Philippi remained faithful, an enduring reminder that faith isn't a fair-weather commitment but a deeply rooted trust in God's promises. This is coupled with the assurance that the good work begun in us will reach a flourishing finish, a hope that provides direction and perseverance.

Lastly, the passage beckons us to live in a manner that makes Jesus Christ attractive to all. It's not just about preaching the word but living it, not just loving much but loving well. It invites us to be bountiful in fruits from the soul, engaging everyone in the glory and praise of God.

We are reminded that our faith journey is not solitary but communal, not static but growing, not just emotional but discerning. It calls us to a life where faith, love, gratitude and hope are not only concepts but lived experiences that draw us closer to the divine and to one another. It's a passage that doesn't just speak to our minds but reaches into our hearts, urging us to be the embodiment of these virtues in a world that continues to long for authentic connections and divine touch.

REFLECTION:

1. Reflecting on the people who have come and gone in your life, those who have been instrumental in shaping who you are – be it for a season, a reason or a lifetime – what aspects of these relationships fill you with gratitude? How has their influence helped you grow in faith and/or love?

2. Paul's writing speaks to an intelligent and sincere love. This isn't about fleeting emotions or surface-level connections; it's about loving with discernment and authenticity. Think of a time when a close friend was making a decision you believed was wrong for them. Rather than simply agreeing to keep the peace, you chose to thoughtfully and honestly express your concerns, valuing the authenticity of the relationship over momentary comfort. Can you identify a moment in your life when you've needed to love someone with this kind of thoughtful sincerity? How did you approach it? What did it teach you about building genuine connections?

3. In the scripture, Paul encourages believers to live in a way that makes Jesus Christ's love visible and attractive to others. This isn't about grand gestures but often about the small, daily choices that reflect sincerity, kindness and wisdom. Think about a recent interaction where you chose patience over anger, understanding over judgment or offered support when it wasn't

convenient for you. How did that choice align with Christ's teachings? How can you continue to make decisions that align with your faith and become a quiet testimony to those around you?

4. This letter to the Philippians is not just a celebration of their faithfulness but a reminder of God's ongoing work in our lives, even through trials. Reflect on a moment when you faced a significant challenge or uncertainty. Perhaps it was a time when you lost a job, faced a health crisis or struggled with a relationship. How did you experience God's presence during this time? How did you find strength in your faith to persevere? What lessons did this experience teach you about trusting God's process and His promise of a flourishing finish?

5. In these verses, we find an invitation to cultivate gratitude, wisdom, love and faithfulness in our daily lives. Consider a particular relationship or situation where you recognize the need for growth in these virtues. It might be your connection with a family member, a challenge at work or a personal goal you're striving to achieve. What specific actions can you take to nurture these qualities? How can you demonstrate more sincere love or make wiser choices? And most importantly, how might these intentional efforts transform that particular relationship or situation and deepen your connection with God and those around you?

6. The scripture describes a 'lover's life' that is passionate and affectionate, cautious, careful, admirable and rich in spiritual fruits. It's a love that goes beyond simple emotions and includes thoughtfulness, integrity and a connection to something greater. Reflect on your relationships, whether with family, friends or others. Can you recall a moment when your love went beyond the ordinary, involving not just affection but also wisdom, discernment or self-sacrifice? How does this deeper, more intentional love compare to the other types of love you have experienced? What might you do to cultivate this kind of love more in your daily life? How could it change the way you connect with others and with God?

PRAYER:

Dear God, I come before You today with a heart brimming with gratitude. Every word in Paul's letter to the Philippians feels like a melody sung just for me, touching the deepest chords of my soul.

Thank You, Lord, for the people You've placed in my life, those who've shaped, supported, and challenged me. I am thankful for the love You've taught me to cultivate, a love that goes beyond fleeting emotions, a love that's intelligent, sincere, discerning and authentic.

Father, help me live each day with a love that reflects Your wisdom and heart. Guide me to make decisions that align with Your teachings so that I may make Christ's love visible to those around me. Show me how to love not just much but well.

In the face of trials and uncertainty, remind me of Your promise to bring to completion the work You've begun in me. Strengthen my faith to trust Your process, knowing that You are faithfully working in my life.

I long to live a 'lover's life,' Lord, one that is cautious, admirable and rich in spiritual fruits. Teach me to love in a way that goes beyond the ordinary, involving affection, wisdom, discernment and self-sacrifice. May my love be a reflection of You.

Fill me with the hope and assurance of Christ's return and guide me in my daily walk so that my life may be bountiful in the fruits of the soul, engaging everyone in Your glory and praise.

I pray all of this in the mighty name of Jesus Christ, my Savior and Lord, who taught me the meaning of true love. Amen.

GOING DEEPER:

1. The scripture talks about being "bountiful in fruits from the soul," The Fruits of the Spirit include love, joy, peace, patience, kindness, goodness, faithfulness, gentleness, and self-control. How are you doing with these fruits? Which are easiest for you to show toward others? Which are more difficult to express? Why do you feel you struggle with some as opposed to others?
2. Imagine your life as a testament to Jesus Christ, just as Paul wished for the Philippians. What would it look like? How might your lifestyle or decisions change if your goal was to make Jesus attractive to everyone you meet?
3. Paul's discerning love is marked by sincerity and intelligence. He didn't just talk about love; he demonstrated it through thoughtful action and honest communication, even when it meant

confronting others about their choices or beliefs. Reflect on a relationship in your life where superficial or polite interactions are taking precedence over authenticity and sincerity. What fears or barriers prevent you from exercising discerning love in this relationship? How might confronting these fears transform the relationship? What specific, practical steps can you take to make the relationship more sincere and authentic, even if it means having uncomfortable or difficult conversations?

4. The Bible reminds us that it's not wrong to feel anger, but we should not sin in our anger. Reflect on the last argument or heated discussion you were in that had the potential to escalate or get "out of control" verbally. How did you respond? How might your reaction have differed from the way Jesus would have handled the situation? Consider the specific attributes of Jesus, such as patience, compassion and forgiveness. What practical steps could you have taken to pull yourself out of the situation and instead reflect these attributes, even when angry? How might this approach change the outcome of the disagreement and serve as a testimony to others of Christ's love and wisdom in your life? Moving forward, how will you actively practice these virtues in daily interactions, turning moments of potential conflict into opportunities to demonstrate Christ's teachings?

5. Many of us have found ourselves relying on "church-speak" or a "church mask," saying phrases like "I'm blessed and highly favored" or "all is well," even when deep inside we're hurting. This practice can impede our growth in virtues like gratitude, wisdom, love and faithfulness and limit the development of authentic relationships. Reflect on a situation where you put on this "mask" rather than being authentic with those around you.
   a. How did that choice affect your relationship with others and with God?
   b. How might it have hindered your growth in a specific virtue?

6. Now, consider how you can cultivate authenticity in your daily interactions, even if it means revealing vulnerability or imperfection.
   a. What steps will you take to foster genuine connections and grow in the chosen virtue?
   b. How do you expect this authenticity to transform your spiritual growth and deepen your relationships within your community, allowing others to know the real you?

NAVIGATING YOUR JOURNEY:

1. Embrace authentic gratitude. Begin each day by reflecting on the blessings in your life. Write them down in a gratitude journal. This practice helps you develop a thankful heart, fostering a deeper connection with God and others.

2. Build community and partnership in faith. Actively seek opportunities to work with others in spreading the Gospel. Join a local church group or community organization. Share your faith

journey and encourage others to do the same. Collaboration in faith deepens our connection and amplifies our ability to make a difference.

3. Develop discerning love. Challenge yourself to grow in love that is not only affectionate but wise and discerning. Practice honesty, thoughtfulness and self-sacrifice in your relationships. Ask for wisdom in loving others the way Christ loves us.

4. Stay faithful through trials. When facing difficulties, remind yourself of God's promises and faithfulness. Lean on your faith community for support, and don't be afraid to seek professional help if needed. Remember, faith is a deeply rooted trust in God's process.

5. Live a life that reflects Christ's love. Think of your daily interactions as opportunities to make Jesus attractive to those around you. Show patience over anger; and understanding over judgment. Your small, everyday choices can become a quiet testimony to others.

6. Remove the "church mask." Cultivate authenticity in your daily interactions. Share your honest feelings with those who have proven themselves trustworthy, even if it reveals your vulnerability or imperfections. Authentic connections allow others to know the real you and help you grow in virtues like wisdom, love and faithfulness. However, remember that being trustworthy is a two-way street. You have to be trustworthy yourself. Respect the confidence and trust that others place in you. This approach fosters deep connections and creates a safe environment where authentic relationships can thrive.

7. Regularly assess how you embody the fruits of the Spirit in your life. Celebrate your growth in areas like love, joy and peace and actively work on areas you struggle with, like patience or self-control. Consider seeking mentorship or guidance in these areas.

Embracing these principles in daily life creates a roadmap for spiritual growth, allowing for a richer connection with God and the community around you. By focusing on gratitude, community, love, faithfulness, reflection, authenticity and self-assessment, you build a fulfilling life that resonates with Christ's teachings. This intentional living not only nurtures your own soul but can serve as a beacon for others, reflecting a faith that is compassionate, wise and deeply rooted.

Day 30: Unwavering Wisdom: Enduring, Seeking and Walking in Love

FOCUS:

Wisdom

SONG:

The Perfect Wisdom of Our God – Keith & Kristyn Getty

INTRODUCTION:

JAMES PRESENTS WISDOM as a much-needed tool to navigate trials, handle temptation, speak thoughtfully and live out a faith that is not just spoken but visibly demonstrated in action. He highlights the transformation that occurs when we welcome God-given wisdom into our lives.

READING:

James 1 (AMP)

James, a bond-servant of God and of the Lord Jesus Christ,

To the twelve [Hebrew] tribes [scattered abroad among the Gentiles] in the dispersion: Greetings (rejoice)!

Consider it nothing but joy, my brothers and sisters, whenever you fall into various trials. Be assured that the testing of your faith [through experience] produces endurance [leading to spiritual maturity, and inner peace]. And let endurance have its perfect result and do a thorough work, so that you may be perfect and completely developed [in your faith], lacking in nothing.

If any of you lacks wisdom [to guide him through a decision or circumstance], he is to ask of [our benevolent] God, who gives to everyone generously and without rebuke or blame, and it will be given to him. But he must ask [for wisdom] in faith, without doubting [God's willingness to help], for the one who doubts is like a billowing surge of the sea that is blown about and tossed by the wind. For such a person ought not to think or expect that he will receive anything [at all] from the Lord, being a double-minded man, unstable and restless in all his ways [in everything he thinks, feels, or decides].

Let the brother in humble circumstances glory in his high position [as a born-again believer, called to the true riches and to be an heir of God]; and the rich man is to glory in being humbled [by trials revealing human frailty, knowing true riches are found in the grace of God], for like the flower of the grass he will pass away. For the sun rises with a scorching wind and withers the grass; its flower falls off and its beauty fades away; so too will the rich man, in the midst of his pursuits, fade away.

Blessed [happy, spiritually prosperous, favored by God] is the man who is steadfast under trial and perseveres when tempted; for when he has passed the test and been approved, he will receive the [victor's] crown of life which the Lord has promised to those who love Him. Let no one say when he is tempted, "I am being tempted by God" [for temptation does not originate from God, but from our own flaws]; for God cannot be tempted by [what is] evil, and He Himself tempts no one. But each one is tempted when he is dragged away, enticed and baited [to commit sin] by his own [worldly] desire (lust, passion). Then when the illicit desire has conceived, it gives birth to sin; and when sin has run its course, it gives birth to death. Do not be misled, my beloved brothers and sisters. Every good thing given and every perfect gift is from above; it comes down from the Father of lights [the Creator and Sustainer of the heavens], in whom there is no variation [no rising or setting] or shadow cast by His turning [for He is perfect and never changes]. It was of His own will that He gave us birth [as His children] by the word of truth, so that we would be a kind of first fruits of His creatures [a prime example of what He created to be set apart to Himself—sanctified, made holy for His divine purposes].

Understand this, my beloved brothers and sisters. Let everyone be quick to hear [be a careful, thoughtful listener], slow to speak [a speaker of carefully chosen words and], slow to anger [patient, reflective, forgiving]; for the [resentful, deep-seated] anger of man does not produce the righteousness of God [that standard of behavior which He requires from us]. So get rid of all uncleanness and all that remains of wickedness, and with a humble spirit receive the word [of God] which is implanted [actually rooted in your heart], which is able to save your souls. But prove yourselves doers of the word [actively and continually obeying God's precepts], and not merely listeners [who hear the word but fail to internalize its meaning], deluding yourselves [by unsound reasoning contrary to the truth]. For if anyone only listens to the word without obeying it, he is like a man who looks very carefully at his natural face in a mirror; for once he has looked at himself and gone away, he immediately forgets what he looked like. But he who looks carefully into the perfect law, the law of liberty, and faithfully abides by it, not having become a [careless] listener who forgets but an active doer [who obeys], he will be blessed and favored by God in what he does [in his life of obedience].

If anyone thinks himself to be religious [scrupulously observant of the rituals of his faith], and does not control his tongue but deludes his own heart, this person's religion is worthless (futile, barren). Pure and unblemished religion [as it is expressed in outward acts] in the sight of our God and Father is this: to visit and look after the fatherless and the widows in their distress, and to keep oneself uncontaminated by the [secular] world.

KEY PRINCIPLES:

1. **Joy Amidst Trials:** Believers should consider it a joy when they face various trials because these challenges refine their faith and produce perseverance, leading to spiritual maturity.
2. **Seeking Wisdom:** If one lacks wisdom, they should confidently ask God, who gives generously. However, asking in faith without doubting God's promise is vital.
3. **Stability of Faith:** Doubt divides a person's loyalty and makes them unstable, akin to a wave of the sea tossed by the wind. A double-minded person should not expect to receive from God.
4. **Temporal Nature of Wealth:** Riches are fleeting, like flowers that wither. It's crucial to find joy in spiritual truths rather than material possessions.
5. **Trials and Temptations:** Trials that test our faith come from God and lead to spiritual rewards. In contrast, temptations to sin arise from personal desires and lead to death.
6. **Source of Goodness:** Every good and perfect gift is from God, the unchanging and eternal light.
7. **Importance of Active Listening:** Believers should be quick to listen, slow to speak and slow to anger. Actions should align with the words of God; merely listening is not enough.
8. **Internalizing God's Word:** Engaging with the word of God shouldn't be a superficial act. Those who hear and act on the word will be blessed.
9. **Control the Tongue:** A key indicator of genuine faith is the ability to control one's speech. The unbridled tongue indicates a heart that is not right with God.
10. **True Religion:** Genuine religion isn't just about rituals but about caring for people in need and the vulnerable. It's also about keeping oneself untainted by the world's corruption.

CONCLUSION:

In the tapestry of life's challenges and the decisions we make, James offers us a beacon of wisdom that is both enlightening and pragmatic. He paints a portrait of a faith that isn't static or merely ritualistic but dynamic, evolving and deeply rooted in the daily grind of our experiences.

As James explains, trials aren't mere obstacles; they are refining fires, shaping and molding our character, leading us toward spiritual maturity. They remind us of the impermanence of material wealth and push us to seek treasures of eternal significance. However, it is not enough to acknowledge trials; we must approach them with an unwavering faith that is undivided in loyalty and singular in its devotion to God.

Temptations, in contrast, are not divine tests but are rooted in our personal desires. They remind us of our humanity and the need to align ourselves with God's will constantly.

But perhaps one of the most profound lessons from James is the emphasis on active, lived faith. The call to be quick listeners, deliberate speakers and slow reactors underscores the importance of introspection in our spiritual journey. It's not just about hearing the Word but living it, ensuring that our external actions mirror our internal convictions.

In this age of fleeting moments and transient emotions, James' message is a clarion call for genuine faith—a faith that cares for the marginalized, controls its speech, and remains untainted by worldly distractions. It beckons us to reflect deeper, act wiser and walk closer with God, offering a roadmap for a meaningful and transformative faith.

REFLECTION:

1. Think about a recent hardship that you experienced. At the time, how did that situation feel to you? What were the lessons you learned from it? Lessons that, when looked back upon the hardship, helped you learn something about yourself or others. Or perhaps lessons that increased your trust or faith or somehow made you stronger – even though the problem you were dealing with was hard?
2. Can you recall a time when you doubted—whether it was your capabilities, decisions or faith in God? How did that doubt affect your actions?
3. Often, doubt breeds fear, and this fear can become so overwhelming that it paralyzes us—leading to what is commonly referred to as 'analysis paralysis.' This state of overthinking can prevent us from taking the necessary steps toward our goals, dreams or desired changes. Have you ever experienced analysis paralysis? How has it potentially hindered you from achieving what you truly wanted or felt called to pursue?
4. Reflect on a moment when you sought solace in buying something, not out of necessity, but to soothe an emotional ache or fill a void. Can you identify the emotion or situation that triggered this 'need to shop'? How did you feel immediately after the purchase? How did those feelings evolve over time? Did you feel the same way about the item after time had passed? Could the funds spent have been used elsewhere in your life? Did whatever you purchased truly address the underlying emotion or situation, or was it just a temporary balm?
5. Recall a conversation where you might have formulated your response before the other person finished speaking. Did your eagerness to reply prevent you from fully understanding or empathizing with what was being shared? How did that impact the conversation and the relationship? Has anyone ever told you, "I just want you to listen, not fix it."? Can you just

listen in that moment, or do you struggle?

6. Reflect on a time when you felt your words ran ahead of your thoughts, causing strain or regret. 'Out of the abundance of the heart, the mouth speaks.' Do you find truth in the idea that your words are a mirror of your heart's state? Delve deeper: Beyond controlling your speech, how often do you inspect the condition of your heart and the emotions or thoughts you harbor?

7. Reflect on any ambitions or desires you've recently pursued. Were any of these driven by a longing for more money, prestige, validation or anything else? As you chased these desires, did you find moments where you were tempted to compromise your values or beliefs, even subtly?

8. Reflect on your religious practices and beliefs. Do you feel they serve as mere rituals, or are they genuinely nurturing your bond with God?

9. The scripture reminds us that genuine religion, as viewed by God, entails looking after the vulnerable and ensuring our own purity from the influences of the secular world. In the context of the age we live in, it's not just about widows and orphans but any individual who is marginalized or faces injustice. There might be voices around you suggesting that everyone should 'pull themselves up by their bootstraps,' but can you identify those who genuinely lack the resources or opportunities to do so?

10. Consider when someone you know - who was once self-reliant - faced sudden challenges, like losing a job or health insurance. Often, it's simple to point fingers at external factors like political entities being the cause. Still, the true essence of life is its unpredictability, which affects everyone irrespective of their affiliation. How do you show your faith in those moments? How is your religion put into action so that others can see it?

PRAYER:

Dear Heavenly Father, in the stillness of this moment, I stand before You, seeking the wisdom and clarity that James so beautifully illuminated. Amid the shifting sands of trials, doubts and temptations, You remain my steadfast anchor, a beacon of unchanging love and grace.

I confess that I've sometimes faltered under the weight of my challenges, questioning their purpose. But I'm reminded today that these trials are not just stumbling blocks. They're refining fires, meticulously shaping my spirit, drawing me ever closer to the image of Your Son. Grant me the joy to embrace them, understanding that they are tools molding my spiritual maturity.

I admit, Lord, to moments of doubt. Times when the vastness of the ocean of life made me feel adrift, questioning even Your presence. In those moments, strengthen my faith. Let me remember the promise of Your generous wisdom, ready to be bestowed upon those who ask with unwavering faith.

Father, in a world so fixated on the fleeting pleasures of wealth and materialism, anchor my heart to the treasures of heaven. May I always prioritize the eternal over the temporal, seeking first Your Kingdom and its righteousness.

As I traverse the path of life, sharpen my ears to be quick to listen, my mind to be slow to anger, and my tongue to utter words that reflect Your heart. And in moments of haste, when words escape without thought, grant me the humility to seek reconciliation and forgiveness and the wisdom to introspect.

Lord, as James has shown, true faith is not merely in rituals or spoken words but in actions and how I treat the vulnerable, marginalized, and forgotten. Kindle in me a burning desire to live out this genuine faith, reflecting Your love in every deed, every word, every silent prayer.

And as life unfolds, with its unpredictability and sudden challenges, teach me to extend a hand of empathy and understanding. May my faith be a personal comfort and a living testament to those around me, drawing them closer to you.

In all things, I seek Your wisdom, Lord. Not just the knowledge of what to do but the deep, transformative understanding of why and how, aligning my every step with Your divine will.

In Jesus' name, I pray. Amen.

GOING DEEPER:

1. Recall the scripture's warning that temptations, arising from our personal desires, can lead us astray and ultimately to undesirable consequences. How do these desires, innocent as they may seem, potentially become a slippery slope toward actions that might not align with your faith or values? Moving forward, how can you ensure that your ambitions are both ethically sound and spiritually grounded and don't become triggers that might lead you astray?

2. James discusses personal desires leading to temptations. In the modern world, there are many lesser-discussed temptations like overeating or the allure of pornography. Rather than focusing on the act itself, what underlying needs or emotions could these acts be attempting to numb or address? How might addressing the root causes help someone build stronger self-control?

3. Our world constantly bombards us with stimuli, from advertisements to content suggesting what we "should" be like or have. How does this bombardment influence our personal desires and potentially our descent into temptation? How can you make better choices about what you take in or use in your everyday life?

4. Our environment and the company we keep can either make us more resilient against temptations or more vulnerable to them. Reflect on your current environment and social

circle. Are there elements that feed into your vulnerabilities? How can you proactively create an environment that strengthens your self-control?

5. Explore how other bible characters faced and dealt with temptation. What can you learn from their experiences? A few examples are as follows:
    a. **Jesus (Matthew 4:1-11):** In the wilderness, Jesus faced temptations from Satan. Each time, Jesus responded with Scripture, demonstrating the power of God's Word in overcoming temptation.
    b. **Joseph (Genesis 39:1-20):** Joseph was tempted by Potiphar's wife, but he chose to flee rather than succumb to sin. This teaches us that sometimes, the best response to temptation is to remove ourselves from the situation entirely.
    c. **David (2 Samuel 11):** Unlike Joseph, King David gave in to temptation when he saw Bathsheba. This resulted in severe consequences, including the death of their child. David's experience teaches us that our actions have consequences and the importance of repentance (Psalm 51) when we fall into sin.
    d. **Eve (Genesis 3:1-6):** Eve was tempted by the serpent in the Garden of Eden to eat the forbidden fruit. Her yielding to temptation led to the fall of humanity, teaching us the far-reaching implications of giving in to temptation.
    e. **Job (Job 1-2):** Job, although facing intense suffering and urged by his wife to "curse God and die," did not yield to this temptation. Instead, he remained faithful, showing us that steadfast faith can withstand even severe trials.

6. Consider moments when you've bottled up emotions only for them to explode later. What underlying heart issues might be contributing to these outbursts? Scripture advises us to guard our hearts diligently, recognizing its profound influence on our actions. How can you actively work on cultivating a more patient, understanding, and forgiving heart, ensuring that even in moments of heightened emotion, your words remain a reflection of grace and wisdom?

7. In your efforts to do "the right things," are you genuinely making a positive impact and nurturing your inner goodness, or are you just occupied with tasks and a "to-do" list? Are you genuinely serving with purpose like Mary, or are you staying busy like Martha?

8. Have you ever considered that the person who once never imagined needing a food pantry might now be swallowing their pride to ask for assistance? Instead of judging or making assumptions based on their past, how can you extend a hand in empathy and understanding? What steps can you take to ensure that your faith and actions are geared toward uplifting those in genuine need, regardless of their previous circumstances? How can you be a beacon of hope and support, ensuring no one feels degraded when life's tides turn against them?

NAVIGATING YOUR JOURNEY:

The quest for wisdom is a lifelong endeavor. Here are some waypoints to assist you:

1. Awareness. Begin by acknowledging your vulnerabilities. Self-awareness is the first step toward growth. Journal your temptations and triggers. Over time, this will help you notice patterns and implement proactive strategies.

2. Daily reflection. Spend 5-10 minutes each evening evaluating your actions and thoughts from the day. Did they align with our faith and values? If not, what adjustments can you make?

3. Limit stimuli. Reduce your exposure to unnecessary stimuli that might feed temptations. This could mean setting app limits, unfollowing certain social media accounts or introducing screen-free hours in your day.

4. Seek accountability. Share your journey with a trusted friend, mentor or counselor. Having someone to check in with can provide motivation and perspective.

5. Surroundings matter. Periodically assess your environment. Consider decluttering spaces, creating quiet corners for reflection and possibly rearranging spots associated with temptation.

6. Choose company wisely. If certain friends or acquaintances consistently lead you toward temptations, it might be time to re-evaluate these relationships. Seek out positive influences who share your values.

7. Dive into scripture. Use Bible stories, as mentioned above, as guiding lights. Ponder, study, and understand how they can apply to your life today.

8. Stay grounded. Consistently remind yourself of your 'why.' When faced with a challenging decision, remember the broader picture and the values that guide your journey.

9. Practice empathy. Always aim to put yourself in the shoes of others. This will help you extend kindness and understanding and avoid quick judgments.

10. Serve actively. Actively seek opportunities to serve and uplift others in your community. This not only aids others but reaffirms your purpose and commitment to your values.

In the intricate dance of life, the steps we take—much like a dancer's—aren't merely influenced by the literal music we hear but by the choices we make, the influences we allow and the values we hold dear. It's not just about the songs that play in our ears but the convictions and beliefs that play in our hearts. By refining these choices and fostering self-awareness, you cultivate a life more attuned to your deepest values. Remember, it's a continuous journey of self-discovery and growth; stay committed, stay true.

Day 31: Day by Day: Trusting God's Leading

FOCUS:

Guidance

SONG:

Show Me – Yolanda Adams

INTRODUCTION:

TODAY, OUR FOCUS IS on seeking divine guidance. The song "Show Me" by Yolanda Adams resonates with our desire to experience God's presence and direction in our lives. We turn to the words of Psalm 25:4-5, where the psalmist passionately seeks God's ways, guidance, and instruction.

For this bonus lesson, you must listen to the song "Show Me" by Yolanda Adams and study the lyrics. If you search the internet for the lyrics, be aware that some sites have incorrect lyrics. But, by listening to the song while reading the lyrics, you will grasp the song's importance to today's reading.

READING:

Psalm 25:4-5 (NIV)

Show me your ways, Lord, teach me your paths. Guide me in your truth and teach me, for you are God my Savior, and my hope is in you all day long.

KEY PRINCIPLES:

1. **Desire for Divine Direction:** Both the scripture and the song convey a deep yearning to understand and follow God's guidance. There's an earnest plea to be shown the ways of the Lord, highlighting the importance of seeking God's will in our lives.

2. **Restoration and Healing:** The song speaks about the transformative power of God, how He takes our brokenness and not just restores but enhances us. This mirrors the trust in God emphasized in the scripture, portraying Him as our savior and beacon of hope.

3. **Reliance on God's Truth:** The Psalmist's request to be guided in God's truth resonates with the song's plea to see God's face. This underscores the theme of seeking genuine encounters with God and adhering to His authentic teachings.

4. **Embracing Vulnerability:** The song delves deep into the concept of vulnerability in God's presence. By laying out our insecurities, fears and hopes before God, we foster a deeper, more intimate relationship with Him, akin to the Psalmist's profound connection.

5. **Enduring Hope:** Both the Psalm and the song encapsulate the idea of sustained hope. Regardless of external circumstances or internal struggles, the unwavering hope in God's guidance and love remains a constant.

6. **Patience and Stillness in Seeking:** While the song talks about waiting and being still to understand God's will, the scripture emphasizes learning God's paths. This principle is about the patience required in our spiritual journey, acknowledging that divine understanding often comes with time and reflection.

7. **Transformation Through Divine Love:** The song's lyrics indicate a change in understanding love after encountering God. This aligns with the scripture's principle of transformative learning under God's teachings, leading to a life more aligned with divine love and understanding.

8. **The Promise of God:** Central to the song and the scripture is the idea of God's promise – His commitment to guide, restore and be present. Holding onto these promises acts as a source of strength and assurance in our spiritual journey.

9. **Teachability:** Both the Psalmist and Yolanda Adams echo a yearning to be shown, taught and

guided by the divine. This principle underscores a humble acknowledgment of our limited understanding and continuous need for God's wisdom. The psalmist's plea for God to "teach me your paths" and the singer's request to "show me Your will" reveal an openness to divine instruction and the transformation that ensues. Such transformation is not just about change but about evolving and becoming better, fortified by a teachable spirit that remains ever eager to grow in the spiritual journey.

CONCLUSION:

In the intricate tapestry of our spiritual journey, the threads of longing, hope and transformation intertwine. The cry of the Psalmist, paired with the heartfelt melodies of Yolanda Adams, paints a portrait of souls yearning for divine guidance. This shared sentiment is not just a fleeting emotion but a foundational desire that echoes across ages and resonates deep within our spirits. Stepping into a space of vulnerability, we are beckoned to openly seek God's wisdom, embracing His transformative love in the process.

It's not about a relentless pursuit of perfection but rather a gentle and earnest endeavor to be molded by the divine craftsman, finding beauty in our imperfections. The continual quest for God's truth, promises, and direction becomes our lives' guiding star. As we reflect on these melodies and verses, let us be reminded that every plea, every tear and every hope placed before God acts as a beacon, drawing us ever closer to His guiding light.

REFLECTION:

1. Reflect on a time when you deeply yearned for guidance. How did you seek answers? Where did you turn for direction?
2. The song touches upon vulnerability and opening up before God. When did you last allow yourself to be truly vulnerable in prayer, laying out your fears, insecurities and hopes?
3. "Show me your ways, Lord." In your daily life, where do you see signs or feel nudges that might be pointing to God's ways for you? How do you respond to them?
4. The promise of God's transformative love is evident in both the scripture and the song. Think of a moment in your life when you felt transformed or uplifted by love—whether divine or human.
5. In the song, there's a shift to understanding love after encountering God. How has your understanding or experience of love evolved through your spiritual journey?
6. The psalmist and Yolanda Adams express patience in seeking God's guidance. How do you practice patience and stillness in moments of uncertainty or when you're seeking answers?

7. Reflecting on the principle of teachability, in which areas of your life do you feel the need for further growth or understanding? How do you remain open to learning and being taught in your spiritual journey?

8. The song mentions being "put back together better than before." Think of a time when you felt broken or fragmented. How did you find healing? And in what ways did that experience make you stronger or more whole?

9. As you consider the theme of divine guidance, what steps can you take in your everyday life to align more closely with God's path and His teachings for you?

PRAYER:

LORD, IN THE QUIET corners of my heart, I find myself yearning, ever so intensely, for Your divine guidance. In the vastness of life, with its myriad challenges and winding paths, I often feel lost, searching for signs of Your hand directing my steps. Today, as I reflect on the Psalmist and the song's heartfelt lyrics, I am reminded that You are ever-present, always ready to show me Your ways.

Yet, Father, there are moments when my vulnerabilities rise, when doubts and insecurities cloud my vision. In those fleeting shadows, grant me the courage to follow through on the path You've laid out for me. Give me boldness, especially in moments when timidity seeks to hold me back. Let me trust You with my tears, fully aware that each one is seen and treasured by You.

In my moments of deepest despair or overwhelming joy, I imagine that You cradle me, much like a newborn; You hold me close to Your heart. There, I feel the rhythm of Your love, a love that doesn't merely heal but elevates, making me better than I was before.

God, I acknowledge that I am but clay in the hands of the Master Potter. Even when I am shattered, whether by my own doing or the actions of others, I trust in Your unmatched ability to mend, shape and make me whole again. Grant me the wisdom to surrender these broken fragments to You, knowing that they will be remade in Your skilled hands, more beautiful and resilient than before.

Show me, Father, how to be patient and still, in the face of uncertainty, trusting that in Your perfect time, all things will fall into place. More than anything, I desire to be teachable and have a spirit that remains eager to learn, grow and evolve under Your coaching. Help me to stay receptive to Your wisdom. As I journey through life, may my heart radiate with the assurance of Your guiding hand, and may every step be a testament to Your boundless love and providence.

In You, I find hope and strength.

In Jesus' name, I pray. Amen.

GOING DEEPER:

1. In seeking God's guidance, we often come face-to-face with our deepest fears and insecurities. What is a fundamental fear or belief that might be hindering your complete surrender to God's guidance? What does this fear stem from? How can you begin to address and heal from this to experience the fullness of God's direction for your life?

2. Teachability implies a willingness to learn and an acknowledgment of one's limitations. How do you respond when divine guidance or spiritual teachings challenge your pre-existing beliefs or values? Are there aspects of your faith where you struggle with humility and teachability?

3. Vulnerability is often seen as a sign of weakness in many societies. Yet, in spiritual contexts, it's a gateway to deeper connections with God. How can you cultivate a culture of vulnerability in your personal life, relationships or community, thereby challenging societal notions? Do you have difficulty asking for help because doing so seems like a sign of weakness to you? If so, why is that?

4. The concept of being "put back together better than before" suggests an idea of rebirth or resurrection. Have there been experiences in your life that felt like a 'death' (whether emotional, relational or spiritual) that subsequently led to a deeper or renewed understanding of yourself or faith? Do you trust God with your 'broken pieces'? Why or why not?

5. The song and the scripture talk about a deep trust in God's plans and timing. Think about a situation where you felt impatient with God's timeline. Maybe it was regarding a relationship, employment, school, health or something else significant...how did this impatience impact your actions, decisions or mindset? What did you learn from the experience?

6. Both the Psalm and the song suggest a transformative power in God's guidance and love. Reflect on any personal transformations you've experienced. Did they come about gently over time, or were they more abrupt – perhaps stemming from a significant life event or revelation? How has this shaped your understanding of God's ways?

7. There's a difference between *knowing* God's will and *actively pursuing* it. In which areas of your life are you simply aware of God's direction but possibly hesitant or resistant to fully embracing it? What barriers or fears hold you back? With today's lesson in mind, realizing that God is ever-present and ready to guide and restore you, how has your perspective shifted? Does understanding His readiness to help, guide and mend you influence your willingness to pursue His direction more actively?

NAVIGATING YOUR JOURNEY:

1. Intentional prayer time. Dedicate specific moments in your day solely for prayer. Start by expressing gratitude, then lay out your concerns and requests for direction. Keeping a prayer journal can help you identify patterns or answers over time.

2. Dive into scripture. The Bible is rich in wisdom. Create a reading plan focusing on passages related to guidance, wisdom and God's promises. Over time, you might find answers in verses you've read multiple times but see in a new light.

3. Cultivate stillness. Find moments in your day, even if just a few minutes, to simply be still and listen. This doesn't mean you'll always hear a direct answer, but cultivating this habit can make you more receptive.

4. Seek wise counsel. Surround yourself with individuals whose relationship with God you respect and admire. Their experiences and insights can provide perspective, and often, God speaks through the wisdom of others.

5. Engage in worship. Music, as today's song exemplifies, has the power to touch our souls deeply. Regularly engage in worship, allowing music to draw you nearer to God and possibly revealing His guidance.

6. Practice reflective journaling. At the end of each day, jot down your experiences, feelings and any signs you believe might be pointing toward God's will. This can help you discern patterns or guidance that weren't immediately obvious.

7. Act on promptings. If you feel nudged to take a certain action or make a specific decision, and it aligns with Scripture and godly wisdom, have the courage to act. God often guides us through promptings in our hearts.

8. Be patient with yourself. Recognize that understanding God's direction can be a process. Celebrate the moments when you do discern His guidance and be compassionate with yourself when you're unsure.

Remember, your journey toward seeking and understanding God's guidance is unique and deeply personal. While challenges will arise, God walks beside you with each step, ready to illuminate your path and offer strength for the journey ahead.

Closing Reflection

———

As you turn the final pages of this journal, I hope you feel enriched and closer to God's profound love for you.

Throughout this 31-day journey, you've explored the principles of guidance, gratitude, and wisdom. Each day has been an invitation, a step toward understanding and aligning with God's will. I trust this path has deepened your understanding, nurturing an appreciation for the subtle and grand ways God's presence weaves into your life.

This book is a foundation, but your spiritual journey is ongoing. As you move forward, know that God's love is ever-present, always waiting to guide and connect with you. Cherish the revelations and lessons from these pages and look ahead with anticipation—the best is yet to come! Thank you for embarking on this journey.

Love,

Yolanda Allen

Don't miss out!

Visit the website below and you can sign up to receive emails whenever Yolanda Allen publishes a new book. There's no charge and no obligation.

https://books2read.com/r/B-A-KIEZ-GEZKC

BOOKS 2 READ

Connecting independent readers to independent writers.

About the Author

Yolanda Allen is a versatile author and entrepreneur based in metro-Atlanta. Originally from Columbia, Missouri, she balances her writing career with her work as a Storage Engineer and her leadership roles within her church community. Recently, Yolanda founded Iris Purple Moon Studio, a digital marketing and brand management firm, and also launched Iris Purple Moon Publishing, which is dedicated to publishing her novels and other innovative projects.

Her upcoming book, "Guidance, Gratitude & Wisdom: A 31-Day Path to Aligning with God's Will," invites readers on a transformative spiritual journey. Although this release focuses on faith, Yolanda's writing also spans psychological thrillers, comedies, horror, and fantasy. Her novels often explore themes of family dynamics, personal growth, and the intricacies of the human experience.

Keep an eye out for Yolanda's future releases under Iris Purple Moon Publishing, promising an eclectic blend of genres and a deep exploration of spirituality and personal growth. Her storytelling continues to touch readers from all walks of life.